BIBLE NAMES Dictionary

Revealing the Character and Authority
of the Names in the Bible

BRUCE D. ALLEN

Still Waters International Missions

ISBN: 978-1-7347189-5-9

PREFACE

The study of Scripture has been a joy and a lifelong endeavor that began when I was only 14. Over the years I have been blessed to sit under the tutelage of many men of God to be challenged with their experience and passion for the word. Much of what they taught me has become a foundation of my continued pursuit of intimacy and wisdom in the study of scripture.

Early on I was thoroughly captivated by a method of study I heard through a brother, Jerry Sundberg, in San Antonio Texas. He would utilize the meanings of the names of places and people in the bible as a launching point for greater insight and revelation.

That method has become one of my favorite methods of study even to this day! What I have compiled here comes from many and various sources over the years which I cannot begin to recall or remember. Some names that do come to mind are E. W. Bullinger, Dr. Judson Cornwall, Yossef Balas, and Priscilla J. Moore to name a few.

What I share here is in response to many who have asked me for a starting point in this process of discovery. I present this work to you with the prayer you also will fall in love once again with Jesus who is the Word and receive deeper and continued insight into the amazing God we serve!

For His Glory,

Bruce Allen

INTRODUCTION

When we study the Bible with an understanding of the meanings of the names of the places and people the scriptures speak of, it gives us an understanding of greater depth. Use this dictionary as you study the Bible, and you will see the scriptures come alive in a new way you have not experienced before.

Greek Word: ὄνομα (ónoma) / Hebrew Word: שֵׁם (shem)

Meaning: In the New Testament, the Greek word ὄνομα (ónoma) goes beyond a mere label or identifier. It carries the essence of the individual or thing it represents. It encompasses reputation, character, and authority. This concept is deeply rooted in the Hebraic understanding of names, where knowing someone's name meant knowing their true nature and essence.

Meaning: In the Old Testament, the Hebrew word שֵׁם (shem) is more than just a label; it is a reflection of one's identity, character, and reputation. Hebrew names often carried prophetic or symbolic meanings, providing insight into the individual's destiny or nature. For example, "Yahweh" (יְהוָה) is the sacred name of God, and it encapsulates His eternal and self-existent nature. Similarly, names like "Isaac" (יִצְחָק) mean "laughter," signifying the joy brought to Abraham and Sarah in their old age.

Understanding the significance of names in both Greek and Hebrew languages enriches our comprehension of biblical texts, as it emphasizes the deep spiritual and symbolic importance attributed to names in the Bible. Names are not mere words; they are vessels of meaning, reflecting the essence, character, and authority of the individuals and places they represent.

Contents

A

Aaron — enlightened; rich; mountaineer

Ab — father, Noah

Abaddon — place of destruction

Abagtha — happy; prosperous

Abana — stony-a river that flows throughout Damascus

Abarim — mountain beyond-a large mountain range in Moab

Abba — papa-an Aramaic word meaning "father"

Abda — servant; worshiper

Abdeel — servant of God

Abdi — servant of God

Abdon — service; servile

AbedNego — servant of Nebo: servant of Ishtar-the name given to Azariah, one of Daniel's three friends

Abel — a breath; vapor; shepherd-the second son of Adam and **Eve Abel** — meadow; brook; stream

AbelBethMaachah — meadow (brook) of the house of **Maacah AbelMaim** — meadow (brook) of waters

AbelMeholah — meadow (brook) of dancing

AbelMizraim — meadow (brook) of the Egyptians

AbelShittim — meadow (brook) of the Acacias

Abez — lofty

Abi — Jehovah is father

Abia — see Abijah

AbiAlbon — father of strength

Abiasaph — my father has gathered

Abiathar — father of preeminence

Abib — ear of corn-the Hebrew month in which the barley

ripened Abida — father of knowledge-also Abidah

Abidah — father of knowledge-also Abida

Abidan — father is judge; my father

Abiel — God is father

Abiezer — father of help

Abigail — father (i.e., cause) of delight

Abihail — father of might

Abihu — he is my father

Abihud — father of honor

Abijah — the Lord is my father-also Abia and Abiah

Abijam — father of the sea (west)-another form of "Abijah"

Abilene — stream; brook

Abimael — my father is God

Abimelech — father of the king

Abinadab — father (source) of generosity (willingness)

Abinoam — father of pleasantness

Abiram — father of elevation

Abishag — my father was a wanderer

Abishai — my father is Jesse; source of wealth

Abishalom — father of peace

Abishua — father of safety (salvation)

Abishur — father of oxen; father is a wall

Abital — father (source) of dew

Abitub — father (source) of goodness

Abiud — father of honor-the Greek form of "Abihud"

Abner — my father of light

Abraham — father of multitudes

Absalom — father of peace-a son of David who tried to usurp the throne from his father

Abyss — no bottom

Accad — fortress

Accho — compressed-a seacoast city located eight miles north of Mount Carmel

Aceldama — field of blood-a field purchased by the priests of Jerusalem from the 30 pieces of silver that bought the betrayal of Jesus

Achaia — trouble-a region of Greece

Achaicus — belonging to Achaia

Achan — trouble

Achar — trouble

Achaz — he holds; he has grasped

Achbor — a mouse

Achim — woes-a shortened form of "Jehoiachim"

Achish — serpent-charmer

Achmetha — a place of horses-the capital of Media

Achor — trouble-a valley south of Jericho

Achsa — serpent-charmer

Achsah — serpent-charmer

Achshaph — sorcery; dedicated

Achzib — false

Adadah — holiday

Adah — pleasure; beauty

Adaiah — pleasing to Jehovah; Jehovah has adorned

Adalia — honor of Ized

Adam — of the ground; firm; red earth man, mankind-the first man Adam — a city near Zaretan

Adama — hearth; red ground

Adami — fortified

Adar — height

Adar — the twelfth month of the Hebrew Year

Adbeel — languishing for God

Addan — stony

Addar — height; honor

Addi — my witness

Ader — a flock-a son of Beriah

Adiel — ornament of God

Adin — ornament

Adina — ornament

Adino — ornament

Adithaim — double crossing; double ornaments

Adlai — lax; weary

Admah — redness; red earth

Admatha — God-given

Adullam — refuge

Aeneas — praise

Aenon — fountains

Agabus — locust

Agag — high; warlike

Agagite — descendant of Agag

Agar — wandering--the Greek word for Hagar

Agate — a stone of translucent quartz

Agee — fugitive

Agrippa — the name of the Roman king of Judea of the Herod family

Agur — gathered

Ahab — father's brother

Ahara — brother's follower

Aharhel — brother of Rachel

Ahasai — my holder; protector

Ahasbai — blooming; shining

Ahava — water-a town in Babylonia

Ahaz — he holds; he has grasped; possessor

Ahaziah — Jehovah holds (sustains)

Ahban — brother of intelligence

Aher — one that is behind

Ahi — my brother

Ahiah — Jehovah is brother

Ahiam — a mother's brother

Ahian — brother of day

Ahiezer — helping brother

Ahihud — brother of honor

Ahijah — brother of Jehovah; Jehovah is brother

Ahikam — my brother has risen

Ahilud — a child's brother; a brother born

Ahimaaz — powerful brother

Ahiman — brother of fortune

Ahimelech — brother of the king; my brother is king

Ahimoth — brother of death

Ahinadab — brother of liberality (willingness)

Ahinoam — pleasant brother

Ahio — his brother

Ahira — brother of evil

Ahiram — exalted brother; any brother is exalted

Ahisamach — supporting brother

Ahishahar — brother of the dawn

Ahishar — brother of song; my brother has sung

Ahithophel — brother of foolishness

Ahitub — a good brother; my brother is goodness

Ahlab — fertile

Ahlai — Jehovah is staying

Ahoah — a brother's reed; brotherly

Ahohite — a descendant of Ahoah

Aholah — tent-woman

Aholiab — a father's tent

Aholibah — my tent is in her

Aholibamah — tent of the high place

Ahumai — heated by Jehovah

Ahuzam — possession

Ahuzzath — holding fast

Ai — heap of ruins

Aiah — a vulture

Aiath — overturned heap of ruins

Aija — heap of ruins

Aijalon — place of gazelles

Aijeleth — gazelle of the morning

Ain — eye; spring

Ajah — a vulture-an alternative spelling for "Aiah"

Ajalon — place of gazelles-an alternative spelling for Aijalon

Akan — intelligent

Akkub — lain in wait; pursuer

Akrabbim — scorpions

Alameth — hiding place-also Alemeth

Alammelech — king's oak

Alemeth — hiding place

Alomoth — virgins

Alemeth   hiding place

Alexander — helper of men

Alexandria — a city of Egypt founded by Alexander the Great

Aliah — sublimity

Alian — sublime

Alleluia — praise ye the Lord

Allon — an oak

AllonBachuth — oak of weeping

Almodad — the agitator

Almon — covering

AlmonDiblathaim — hiding place of two fig sacks-an Israelite encampment

Alphaeus — leader; chief

Altaschith — destroy not

Alush — crowd

Alvah — sublimity

Alvan — sublime

Amad — enduring

Amal — laboring

Amalek — warlike; dweller in the vale

Amalekites — a people against whom the Israelites often fought

Amam — gathering place

Amana — forth

Amariah — Jehovah has said

Amasa — burden-bearer; people of Jesse

Amasai — burden-bearer

Amashai — carrying spoil

Amasiah — Jehovah bears; Jehovah has strength

Amaziah — Jehovah has strength

Amen — verily; so be it-used to express assent or approval

Ami — (meaning uncertain)

Aminadab — my people are willing (noble)-the Greek for of

Amminadab Amittai — truthful

Ammah — head

Ammi — my people

Ammiel — my people are strong; my kinsman is God

Ammihud — my people are honorable or glorious

Amminadab — my people are willing or noble

Amminadib — my people are liberal

AmmiShaddai — the Almighty is my kinsman; my people are mighty

Ammizabad — my people are endowed; my kinsman has a present

Ammon — a people; inbred-Lot's son by his youngest daughter)

Ammonites — descendants of Ammon

Amnonup — bringing; faithful

Amok — deep

Amon — workman

Amorites — mountain dwellers

Amos — burden-bearer; burdensome

Amoz — strong, strength

Amphipolis — surrounded city

Amplias — large

Amram — people exalted; red

Amramites — descendants of Amram

Amraphel — powerful people

Amulet — charm worn to protect wearer against evil or to aid him

Amzi — my strength

Anab — grape

Anah — answering

Anaharath — gorge

Anaiah — Jehovah has covered; Jehovah answers

Anak — giant; long necked

Anakim — descendants of Anak; a race of giants

Anamim — rock men

Anammelech — Anu is king

Anan — he beclouds, cloud

Anani — my cloud

Ananiah — Jehovah is gracious

Ananias — Jehovah is gracious

Anarchy — state of lawlessness or disorder due to the absence of govern- mental authority

Anath — answer

Anathema — denunciation of something as accursed

Anathoth — answers; answered prayer

Andrew — manly, conqueror

Andronicus — conqueror

Anem — two fountains

Aner — sprout; waterfall

Anethothite — a native of Anathoth

Angel — agent; messenger-Supernatural being created by God before mankind

Aniam — lamentation of the people

Anim — fountains

Anise — a plant used for seasoning and medicinal purposes; dill

Anna — grace

Annas — grace of Jehovah

Anon — at once; immediately

Antediluvians — those who lived before the flood

Antioch of Pisidia — speedy as a chariot-a city in Pisidia

Antioch of Syria — speedy as a chariot-a city in Syria

Antipatris — for his father

Antothijah — answers

Antothite — a native of Anathoth of Jehovah; belonging to

Anathoth Anub — strong; high

Apelles — meaning uncertain

Apharsachites — investigator-an unknown people, possibly part of an Assyrian tribe that settled in Samaria

Aphek — strength

Aphekah — fortress

Aphiah — striving

Aphik — strength

Aphrah — house of dust

Aphses — the dispersed

Apocrypha — hidden; secret things

Apollonia — city of Apollo

Apollos — a destroyer

Apollyon — the destroyer

Apostle — send forth

Apothecary — pharmacist; perfumer

Appaim — face; presence; nostrils

Appii Forum — marketplace of Appius-a town about 40 miles south of Rome

Apple of the Eye — a figurative expression for something very valuable

Aquila — eagle-Jewish Christian; husband of Priscilla and friend of Paul

Ar — city

Ara — strong

Arabah — desert plain, steppe

Arabia — desert-a large peninsula bounded on the east by the Persian Golf and the Fulf of Oman, on the West by the Red Sea, and on the south by the Indian Ocean

Arabian — dusk, evening, desert

Arad — fugitive; wild ass

Arah — wayfarer

Aram — high; exalted

Aramaic — Semitic language related to Hebrew

AramNaharim — an area in northern Mesopotamia

Aran — firmness

Ararat — high land-mountainous land in eastern Armenia (modern Turkey)

Aratus — a Greek poet who lived about 270 B.C.

Araunah — Jehovah is firm

Arba — four; strength of Baal

Arbah — a region in early Palestine

Arbathite — a native of Betharabah

Arbite — a native of Arab

Archelaus — people's chief

Archevites — people settled in Samaria during exile

Archippus — chief groom

Archite — the long

Arcturus — a constellation called the Bear

Ard — sprout; descent

Ardon — descendant

Areli — valiant; heroic; God's hearth

Arelites — of the family of Areli

Areopagite — a member of the court

Areopagus — hill of Ares (Mars)-a hill west of the Acropolis in Athens

Aretas — pleasing; virtuous

Argob — region of clods

Aridai — delight of Hari

Aridatha — given by Hari

Arieh — lion of Jehovah

Ariel — lion of God (affectionate name for Jerusalem)

Arimathea — heights-city believed to have been located in western Ephraim

Arioch — lion-like

Arisai — (meaning uncertain)

Aristarchus — the best ruler

Aristobulus — the best counselor

Arkite — belonging to Arka

Armageddon — hill of Megiddo

Armenia — land southeast of the Black Sea; Ararat

Armoni — of the palace

Arnan — joyous; strong

Arnon — rushing water; flood-a river that pours into the Dead Sea

Arod — descent; posterity

Aroer — naked

Aroerite — a descendant of Aroer

Arpad — strong(hold); spread out

Arphaxad — (meaning uncertain)

Artaxerxes — fervent to spoil

Artemas — whole, sound

Artemis — the mother-goddess of Asia Minor

Aruboth — windows

Arumah — heights

Arvad — wandering

Arvadites — inhabitants of Arvad

Arver — nudity; nakedness

Arza — firm

Asa — physician; healer

Asahel — God is doer; God has made

Asaiah — Jehovah is doer; Jehovah has made

Asaph — collector; gatherer; recorder

Asareel — God is joined or ruler

Asarelah — Jehovah is joined; whom God has bound

Asenath — dedicated to (the deity) Neith

Aser — happy-see Asher

Ashan — smoke-a town probably located northwest of Beersheba

Ashbea — man of Baal

Ashbel — man of Baal

Ashchenaz — a fire that spreads

Ashdod — stronghold; ravager; robber

AshdothPisgah — springs of Pisgah; springs of the fortress

Asher — happy-see Aser

Asherah — a goddess of the Phoenicians and Arameans

Ashima — heaven

Ashkelon — wandering

Ashkenaz — a fire that spreads

Ashnah — hard, firm

Ashpenaz — meaning uncertain

Ashriel — God is joined; vow of God

Ashtaroth — plural of Astoreth-also Astaroth

AshterothKarmain — Ashtaroth of the two horns

Ashtoreth — name given by the Hebrews to the goddess

Ashtart (Astarte) Ashur — free man; man of Horus

Ashvath — made; wrought

Asiel — God is doer or maker

Askelon — see Ashkelon (wandering)

Asnah — thornbush

Asnapper — believed to have been Ashurbanipal, king of

Assyria Aspatha — horse-given

Asriel — God is joined; vow of God

Asshur — level plain

Asshurim — mighty ones

Assir — prisoner

Assos — approaching-a seaport of Mysia in Asia Minor

Assur — see Asshur

Assyria — to go forth; be sent forth with success; captivity-country of Assur; a Semitic nation of the Tigris River, whose capital was Nineveh

Astaroth — see Ashtaroth

Asuppim — gatherings; stores

Asyncritus — incomparable

Atad — a thorn

Atarah — crown; ornament

Ataroth — crown

AtarothAddar — crown of Addar

Ater — bound; lame

Athach — stopping place

Athaiah — Jehovah is helper

Athaliah — whom Jehovah has afflicted; Jehovah is strong

Attai — timely

Attalia — seaport town of Pamphylia named after Attalus II

Augustus — emporer of Rome at time of Christ's birth

Ava — legion-Assyrian city

Aven — nothingness

Avim — villagers

Avites — see Avim

Avith — ruins

Aza — noble; slope

Azaliah — Jehovah is noble

Azaniah — Jehovah is hearer

Azareel — God is helper

Azarel — see Azareel

Azariah — Jehovah has helped

Azaz — strong; powerful

Azaziah — Jehovah is strong

Azbuk — pardon

Azekah — dug up place-city southwest of Jerusalem

Azel — noble-a descendant of King Saul

Azem — bone see Ezem

Azgad — worship; supplication; God is strong

Aziel — God is determining

Aziza — strong

Azmaveth — council or strength of death

Azmon — strong

AznothTabor — peaks (ears) of Tabor

Azor — helper

Azotus — stronghold

Azriel — God is helper

Azrikam — my help has risen

Azubah — forsaken

Azur — helper; helpful-see Azzur

Azzur — see Azur

Azzah — strong-southernmost of five shief Philistine cityes; same as Gaza

Azzan — sharp; thorn

B

Baal — master; lord-the most important of the Canaanite gods; male coun- terpart to Ashtaroth

Baalah — mistress

Baalath — mistress

BaalathBeer — mistress of a well

BaalBerith — lord of the covenant

Baale — mistress

BaalGad — the lord of fortune; Gad is Lord

BaalHamon — lord of a multitude

BaalHanan — the lord is gracious

BaalHazor — lord of Hazor (enclosure)

BaalHermon — lord of Hermon

Baali — my master (lord)

Baalim — lords-plural of Baal

BaalMeon — lord of the house

BaalPeor — lord of Mount Peor

BaalPerazim — lord of breaches

BaalShalisha — lord of a third part

BaalTamar — lord of palms

BaalZebub — lord of the

BaalZephon — lord of the North

Baana — son of grief; patient

Baanah — son of grief; affliction

Baara — a wood; the burning one

Baaseiah — Jehovah is bold

Babel — gate of God

Babylon — a city situated on banks of the Euphrates river; capital of Babylonian empire

Baca — weeping

Bahurim — low ground

Bajith — house

Bakbakkar — diligent; searcher

Bakbuk — waste; hollow

Bakbukiah — wasted by Jehovah

Balaam — a pilgrim; lord (Baal) of the people-a prophet under the king of Moab

Balac — see Balak

Baladan — having power

Balah — mistress

Balak— void; empty-see Balac

Bamah — high place

Bamoth — high places

BamothBaal — high places

Bani — posterity

Barabbas — father's son

Barachel — blessed of God

Barachias — blessed of Jehovah

Barak — lightening

Barhumite — another form of Baharumite; an inhabitant of

Bahurim Bariah — fugitive

BarJona — son of Jonah

Barkos — partly colored

Barnabas — son of consolation

Barsabas — son of Saba

Bartholomew — son of Tolmai

Bartimaeus — honorable son-son of Timaeus

Baruch — blessed

Barzillai — strong

Bashan — fertile plain-district stretching from the Upper Jordan Valley to the Arabian Desert known for fine cattle/oaks

Bashemath — fragrant

Basmath — fragrant

BathRabbim — daughter of multitudes

BathSheba — the seventh daughter; daughter of the oath

BathShua — daughter of prosperity

Bavai — wither

Bazluth — asking

Bealiah — Jehovah is lord

Bealoth — mistresses; possessors

Bebai — fatherly

Becher — youthful; firstborn

Bechorath — first birth

Bedad — alone

Bedan — son of judgment

Bedeiah — servant of Jehovah

Beeliada — the Lord knows

Beelzebub — chief of the devils

Beer — a well

Beera — expounder

Beerah — expounder

BeerElim — well of heroes

Beeri — man of the springs; expounder

BeerLahaiRoi — well of the living one who sees me

Beeroth — wells

BeerSheba — well of oaths

Beeshterah — temple of Ashterah

Bel — name for Babylonian sun god Marduk

Bela — destroying-see Belah

Belial — useless; without worth

Belshazzar — Bel has protected the king(ship)

Belteshazzar — protect his life

Ben — son

Benaiah — Jehovah has built

BenAmmi — son of my people

BeneBerak — sons of lightning

BeneJaakan — the children of Jaakan

BenHadad — son of (the god) Hadad

BenHail — strong; son of strength

BenHanan — son of grace

Beninu — our son

Benjamin — son of the right hand

Beno — his son

BenOni — son of my sorrow

BenZoheth — son of Zoheth; corpulent; strong

Beon — house of On

Beor — shepherd-see Bosor

Bera — gift

Berachah — blessing

Beraiah — unfortunate

Berea — watered

Berechiah — Jehovah is blessing

Bered — hail

Beri — expounded

Beriah — unfortunate

Berith — covenant

Bernice — victorious

BerodachBaladan — same as Merodach obaladan

Berothah — of a well-see Berothai

Besai — treading down

Besodeiah — given to trust in Jehovah

Besor — cold

Betah — confidence

Beten — valley

Beth — house

Bethabara — house at the ford

Bethanath — house of reply; house of Anath

Bethanoth — house of reply; house of Anoth

Bethany — house of affliction; place of unripe figs

Betharabah — house of the desert

Betharam — house of the heights

Betharbel — house of ambush

Bethaven — house of idols

Bethazmaveth — house of Azmaveth

Bethbarah — house of the ford

Bethbirei — house of my creation

Bethcar — house of the lamb

Bethdagon — house of Dagon

Bethdiblathaim — house of fig cakes

Bethel — house of God

Bethemek — house of the valley

Bether — separation

Bethesda — house of outpouring or overflowing water

Bethezel — a place near

Bethgader — house of walls

Bethgamul — camel house

Bethhaccerem — house of vines

Bethharam — mountain house

Bethhogla — partridge house

Bethhoglah — partridge house

Bethhoron — cave house

Bethjeshimoth — house of deserts

Bethlebaoth — house of lionesses

Bethlehem — house of bread

Bethmaachah — house of Maacah

Bethmarcaboth — house of chariots

Bethmeon — house of habitation

Bethnimrah — house of leopardess

Bethpalet — house of escape

Bethpazzez — house of dispersion

Bethpeor — house of Peor

Bethphage — house of unripe figs

Bethphelet — house of escape

Bethrapha — house of a giant

Bethrehob — house of Rehob (breath)

Bethsaida — fish house

Bethshemesh — house of the sun

Bethshittah — house of acacia

Bethtappuah — house of apricots

Bethuel — dweller of God

Bethzur — house of rock

Betonim — bellies; pistachio nuts

Beulah — married

Bezai — shining; high

Bezaleel — God is protection

Bezek — sowing

Bezer — fortress

Bichri — youth; firstborn

Bidkar — servant of Ker (Kar)

Bigtha — given by fortune

Bigthan — given by fortune

Bigthana — given by fortune

Bigvai — happy; of the people

Bildad — lord Adad; son of contention

Bileam — foreigners

Bilgah — bursting forth; firstborn

Bilgai — bursting forth

Bilhah — tender

Bilhan — tender

Bilshan — searcher

Bimhal — circumcised

Binea — wanderer

Binnui — being a family

Birsha — thick; strong

Birzavith — olive well

Bishlam — peaceful

Bithiah — daughter of Jehovah

Bith-ron — ravine

Bithyni — a violent rainfall

Bizjothjah — contempt of Jehovah

Biztha — eunuch

Blains — blisters full of pus

Blastus — a bud

Boanerges — sons of thunder

Boaz — fleetness; strength

Bocheru — youth

Bochim — weepers

Bohan — stumpy

Booz — see Boaz

Boscath — Bozcath

Bosor — a lamp

Bowels — intestines; seat of pity, tenderness, or courage

Bozez — shining

Bozkath — craggy-see also Boscath

Bozrah — enclosure; fortress; stronghold-a city of Edom; famous for their dyed garments

Brook of Willows — (as in weeping willows) It was on the willows where Is- rael hung their harps (the harp being symbolic of the heart)

Bukki — proved of Jehovah; mouth of Jehovah

Bukkiah — proved of Jehovah; mouth of Jehovah

Bul — growth

Bunah — understanding

Buz — contempt

Buzi — despised by Jehovah

Buzite — belonging to Buz

C

Cabbon — understanding

Cabul — displeasing; obscurity

Caesar — formal title for Roman emperors

Caesarea — city of Caesar

Cage — a barred cell for confining prisoners

Caiaphas — depression

Cain — acquired, spear

Cainan — acquired

Calah — old age

Calamus — sweet cane

Calcol — sustaining; nourishment

Caldron — a large kettle

Caleb — impetuous; raging with madness

Calker — a sealer

Calneh — fortress

Calvary — from the Latin "calvaria" (skull)

Camel — humpbacked animal used as draft and saddle beast

Camon — elevation

Camp — to pitch a tent; site on which tents are erected

Camphire — henna; a fragrant shrub

Cana of Galilee — reeds

Canaan — low

Canaan, Land of — "purple"-native name of Palestine

Canaanites — original inhabitants of Canaan

Candace — "contrite one"-dynastic title of Ethiopian queens

Candle — a light; lamp

Candlestick — a stand for lamps; the Menorah

Cane — a tall, sedgy grass

Canker — a spreading sore; an erosion

Cankerworm — insect larvae that destroys plants by feeding on them

Canneh — "distinguished"—a town on the southern coast of Arabia

Capernaum — "village of Nahum"-a town on the northwest shore of the Sea of Galilee

Caph — eleventh letter of Hebrew alphabet

Caphtor — isle

Cappadocia — "five horses"-aprovince of Asia Minor

Carbuncle — a precious gem

Carcas — severe

Carchemish — city (fortress) of Chemosh

Careah — bald head

Carmel — orchard; a plant; field; garden; fruitful field-where Elijah brought Israel back to Jehovah and slew the prophets of foreign gods

Carmelite — native of Judean Carmel

Carmi — fruitful; noble

Carmites — family of Judah whose head was Carmi

Carob pod — seedcase of the carob; locust tree

Carpus — fruit; wrist

Carriage — ancient means of transportation; archaic word for baggage

Carshena — distinguished; lean

Casement — lattice; criss-crossed strips of wood or metal

Casiphia — silvery

Casluhim — a descendant of Ham

Cassia — amber; an aromatic wood

Castaway — worthless; reprobate

Caste — divisions of society

Castor and Pollux — sons of Jupiter

Caul — a lining surrounding the stomach; a hair net worn by women

Cedron — obscure; making black or dad-a valley in Jerusalem

Cenchrea — millet

Censer — firpan; vessel for burning incense

Cephas — the stone

Chaff — the husk of threshed grain

Chacedony — from Chalcedon

Chalcol — sustaining-a wise man with whom Solomon was compared

Chaldea — demons

Chaldeans — known for their intellectual prowess, astrology, stargazing, sorcery, etc.; those living in Chaldea-also Chaldees

Chambering — sexual excesses

Chamberlain — chief officer in the home of a king or nobleman

Chapiter — top of a post or column

Chapman — a merchant

Charashim — ravine of craftsmen

Charran — mountains-Mesopotamian city; same as Haran

Chebar — strength

Chedorlaomer — servant of (the goddess) Lakamar

Chelal — completeness

Chelluh — robust

Chelub — boldness

Chelubai — impetuous; raging with madness

Chemarim — servants; priests

Chemosh — fire; hearth-a god of Moab

Chenaanah — flat; low

Chenani — Jehovah; creator

Chenaniah — established by Jehovah

ChepharHaammonai — village of the Ammonites

Chephirah — town

Cheran — lyre; lamb; union

Cherethites — Cretans in southwest Palestine

Cherith — trench-a brook in the Transjordan

Cherubim — an angelic order

Chesalon — hopes

Chesed — gain

Chesil — fool

Chesulloth — loins

Chezib — false

Chidon — javelin

Chileab — restraint of father

Chilion — pining

Chilmad — closed

Chimham — pining

Chinnereth — harps

Chios — open

Chisleu — ninth month of Hebrew year

Chislon — strength

ChislothTabor — loins of tabor

Chiun — detestable thing

Chloe — a tender sprout

Choler — anger

ChorAshan — smoking furnace-town in Judah given to Simeon

Chorazin — secret-a coastal city of the Sea of Galilee

Chozebaun — truthful

Christ — the Anointed One

Chronicles — the word of the days-two books of the Old Testament **Chrysolite** — gold stone

Chrysoprasus — golden-green stone

Chub — a textual variant of Lub (Libya)

Chun — founding

Church — all who have been redeemed; also refers to groups of Christians assembled for worship

Churl — a rude, surly person

ChusanRishathaim — man of Cush; he of twofold crime

Chuza — seer

Cilicia — rolling-a province of Asia Minor

Cinnamon — a laurel-like spicy plant

Cis — Greek form of Kish, father of King Saul

Clauda — lamentable

Claudia — lame

Claudius — lame ruler-a Roman emperor (reigned 41-54 AD)

Claudius Lysias — lame dissolution

Clement — mild

Cleopas — renowned father

Cleophas — renowned

Cnidus — age

Cockatrice — type of venomous snake

Cockle — stinging weeds

ColHozeh — wholly a seer

Collops — a slice of meat

Colossae — punishment

Conaniah — Jehovah has founded-a Levite appointed to be overseer of tithes and offerings at the temple

Concision — mutilation

Concupiscence — sinful desire

Condescend — to descend to or humble oneself to the level of others

Coniah — Jehovah establishes

Cononiah — Jehovah has founded

Core — the Greek form of "Korah"

Coriander — a plant whose seed is compared to manna

Corinth — a city in Greece

Cormorant — an unclean bird

Cosam — a diviner

Cotes — a small coop or shed for keeping domestic animals

Coulter — a mattock or plowshare

Coz — thorn; nimble

Cozbi — deceitful

Crescens — increasing

Crete — carnal-an island in the Mediterranean Sea

Crispus — curled

Cumi — an Aramaic word meaning "arise"

Cummin — an annual of the parsley family

Cush — black

Cushi — black

Cuth — burning-see Cuthah

Cyrene — wall

Cyrenius — of Cyrene

Cyrus — sun; throne

D

Dabareh — pasture-a city of Issachar

Dabbasheth — camel hump

Daberath — pasture-a city of Issachar

Dagon — fish

Dalaiah — Jehovah is deliverer

Daleth — the fourth letter in the Hebrew alphabet

Dalmanutha — bucket

Dalmatia — deceitful

Dalphon — swift

Dam — mother (used of a domestic animal)

Damaris — heifer

Damascus — sackful of blood-chief city of Aram Danjudge

Daniel — God is my judge

DanJaan — judgement

Dannah — judging

Darda — bearer (pearl) of wisdom

Darius — he that informs himself

Darkon — carrier

Darling — only one

Dathan — front

David — beloved

Debir — oracle

Deborah — bee

Decapolis — ten cities

Dedan — low

Dedication, Feast of — Hanukkah; commemorates the victories of Judas Maccabeus and the purification and rededication of the Temple.

Dehavites — people who settled in Samaria during the exile

Dekar — lancer

Delaiah — Jehovah has raised; Jehovah is deliverer

Delilah — longing; dainty one

Demagogue — one who becomes a leader by exploiting mas prejudice or sentiment

Demas — popular

Demetrius — belonging to Demeter

Demon — an evil spirit

Derbe — sting-a city of Lycaonia

Diblaim — two cakes; double embrace

Diblath — round cake

Dibon — wasting (away); pining

DibonGad — wasting of God-a halting place of the Israelites leaving Egypt

Dibri — eloquent; on the pasture born

Didymys — twin

Diklah — place of palms

Dilean — cucumber

Dimnah — dung heap

Dimon — riverbed; pining, wasting away

Dimonah — wasting

Dinah — judgement

Dinhabah — give judgement

Dionysius — of the (god) Dionysos

Diotrephes — nourished by Jupiter

Dishan — antelope; leaping

Dishon — antelope; leaping

Dizahab — have gold

Dodai — beloved

Dodanim — decendants of Javan

Dodavah — loved of Jehovah

Dodo — beloved

Doeg — anxious; cared for

Dophkah — drover

Dor — dwelling

Dorcas — gazelle

Dothan — two wells

Drams — gold coins of Persia, weighing about 3.4 grams

Dromedary — a species of camel; a swift steed

Drusilla — watered by dew

Dulcimer — a stringed musical instrument

Dumah — deep silence-a city of Edom

Dura — fortress

E

Ebal — stone, bare

Ebed — servant

EbedMelech — the king's servant

Ebenezer — stone of help

Eber — the region beyond-see Heber

Ebiasaph — the father has gathered

Ebronah — passage; opposite

Ed — witness

Edar — flock

Eden — delight; pleasure

Eder — flock-same as Edar

Edom — red; earthy

Edomites — descendants of Esau

Edrei — fortress

Eglah — calf

Eglaim — pond; double fountain-the word being the plural of calf and de- picts two frisky calves

Eglon — of a calf

Egypt — land of the soul of Ptah-the land of the Nile in the northeast corner of Africa

Ehi — exalted brother; my brother is exalted

Ehud — strong

Eker — root

Ekron — migration

El — ancient word for God; often used as a part of Hebrew names

Eladah — God is ornament

Elah — oak

Elam — hidden-a personification of the empire of south Iran; the Elamites

Elamites — descendants of Elam

Elasah — God is doer

Elath — terebinth tree-see Eloth

ElBethel — God of Bethel

Eldaah — God has called

Eldad — God is a friend

Elead — God is witness

Elealeh — God has ascended

Eleasah — God has made

Eleazar — God is helper

ElEloheIsrael — God, the God of Israel

Eleph — ox

Elhanan — whom God gave; God is gracious

Eli — my God-see Eloi

Eli — Jehovah is high

Eliab — God is father

Eliada — God is knowing

Eliah — Jehovah is my God

Eliahba — God conceals

Eliakim — God will establish

Eliam — my God is a kinsman; God is founder of the people

Elias — see Elijah

Eliasaph — God is gatherer

Eliashib — God is requiter

Eliathah — God is come

Elidad — God is a friend

Eliel — God, my God

Elienai — unto God are my eyes

Eliezer — God is help

Elihoenai — to Jehovah are my eyes

Elihoreph — God of harvest grain

Elihu — God himself

Elijah — Jehovah is my God

Elika — God is rejector

Elim — oaks

Elimelech — my God is King

Elioenai — to Jehovah are my eyes

Eliphal — God is judge

Eliphalet — see Eliphelet

Eliphaz — God is dispenser

Elipheleh — Jehovah is distinction

Eliphelet — God is escape-see Eliphalet

Elisabeth — God is swearer; oath of God

Elisha — God is Savior-see Eliseus

Elishah — God is Savior

Elishama — God is hearer

Elishaphat — God is judge

Elisheba — God is swearer; God is an oath

Elishua — God is hearer

Eliud — God my praise

Elizabeth — see Elisabeth

Elizaphan — God is protector

Elizur — God is a rock

Elkanah — God is possessing

Elkoshite — an inhabitant of Elkosh

Ellasar — oak

Elmodam — measure

Elnaam — God is pleasant

Elnathan — God is giving

Eloi — see Eli (cry of Jesus)

Elon — oak, strong

ElonBethHanan — oak of the house of grace

Elonites — belonging to Elon

Eloth — see Elath

Elpaal — God is working

Elpalet — God is escape

ElParan — oak of Paran

Eltekeh — grace

Eltekon — founded by God

Eltolad — kindred of God

Elul — vine

Eluzai — God is strong

Elymas — a sorcerer-son of Joshua

Elsabad — God is endowing

Elzaphan — God is protector

Emim — terrors

Emmanuel — a name of Jesus

Emmaus — despised people

Emmor — Greek form of Hamor

Enam — double fountains

Enan — eyes; fountain

EnDor — fountain of habitation

EnEglaim — fountain of two calves

EnGannim — fountain of gardens

EnGedi — fountain of the goat

EnHaddah — flowing strongly

EnHakkore — well of the one who called

EnHazor — fountain of the village

EnMishpat — fountain of judgement

Enoch — teacher

Enos — mortal-see Enosh

EnRimmon — fount of pomegranates

Enrogel — fuller's fountain

EnShemesh — eye of the sun

Entappuah — fountain of the apple tree

Epaenetus — praiseworthy-see Epenetus

Epaphras — lovely

Epaphroditus — lovely

Ephah — obscurity

Ephah — a dry measure, equal to approximately one bushel

Ephai — obscuring

Epher — calf; young deer

EphesDammim — boundary of blood

Ephesus — desirable-a town on the western coast of Asia Minor; an impor- tant trading center

Ephlal — judgement

Ephod — a vest

Ephphatha — be opened

Ephraim — fruitful

Ephraimite — descendant of Ephraim

Ephrain — hamlet

Ephratah — fruitfulness; same as Bethlehem-see Ephrath

Ephrathite — inhabitant of Bethlehem

Ephron — strong

Epicureans — followers of Epicurus

Er — watcher

Eran — watcher; watchful

Erastus — beloved

Erech — length

Eri — watcher

Erites — the family of Eri

Esaias — the Greek word for Isaiah-see Isaiah

EsarHaddon — Ashur has given a brother

Esau — hairy-the eldest son of Isaac, and Jacob's twin brother

Esek — strife

EshBaal — man or servant of Baal

Eshban — man of understanding

Eshcol — a cluster of grapes

Eshean — support

Eshek — oppressor

Eshkalonites — natives of Ashkelon

Eshtaol — way

Eshtaulites — inhabitants of Eshtaol

Eshtemoa — bosom of women-see Eshtemoh

Eshton — rest

Esli — reserved

Esrom — see Hezron

Esther — star; (the goddess) Ishtar

Etam — wild beast's lair

Etham — sea-bound

Ethan — ancient

Ethanim — seventh month in the Hebrew year-see Tishri

Ethbaal — Baal's man; with Baal

Ether — plenty

Ethiopia — burnt face

Ethiopians — descendants of Cush-residents of Ethiopia

Ethnan — gift

Ethni — my gift

Eubulus — of good counsel

Eunice — conquering well

Eunuch — castrated man employed as a royal official

Euodias — fragrant

Euphrates — that which makes fruitful; to breakforth; rushing

Euroclydon — east wind

Eutychus — fortunate

Eve — life; life-giving-the first woman; Adam's wife

Evi — desire

EvilMerodach — the man of (the god) Marduk

Ezar — see Ezer

Ezbai — shining; beautiful

Ezbon — bright

Ezekias — Jehovah is strength-see Hezekiah

Ezekiel — God strengthens

Ezel — division; separation

Ezem — bone

Ezer — help

Ezion-Geber — giant's backbone-also Ezion-Gaber

Eznite — spear; to be sharp

Ezra — help

Ezrahite — belonging to Ezrach

Ezri — my help

F

Felix — happy

Felloes — obsolete word meaning rims

Festus — swine-like; successor of Felix

Firebrand — to rake together (embers); a poker

Fitches — vetches; tares

Fortunatus — fortunate

Fuller's (field) — to trample with the foot; wash

G

Gaal — rejection

Gaash — earthquake

Gaba — hill

Gabbai — collector

Gabbatha — pavement

Gabriel — man of God-an angel

Gad — fortune

Gadarenes — people from the area of Gadara

Gaddi — my fortune

Gaddiel — fortune of God

Gadi — fortunate

Gadite — an inhabitant of Gad

Gaham — blackness

Gahar — prostration; concealment

Gaius — lord

Galal — great; rolling

Galatia — land of Galli-a province of central Asia Minor

Galatians — people of Galatia

Galbanum — a yellowish brown aromatic resin

Galeed — heap of witness

Galilean — an inhabitant of Galilee

Galilee — circle; (full) circuit-large Roman district of Palestine and primary region of Jesus' ministry

Gallim — heaps

Gallio — who lives on milk

Gamaliel — reward or recompense of God

Gammadim — warriors

Gamul — weaned

Gareb — reviler; despiser

Garmite — bony

Gashmu — rain storm; corporealness-an anemy of the Jews who opposed them upon their return from the Exile

Gatam — burnt valley

Gath — wine press

GathHepher — wine press of digging

GathRimmon — pomegranate press

Gaza — strong

Gazer — dividing-Canaanite town beside the Mediterranean Sea

Gazez — shearer

Gasites — see Gazathites

Gazzam — devourer; swaggerer

Geba — hill; small hill

Gebal — mountain

Geber — man; strong one

Gebim — ditches; cisterns

Gedaliah — Jehovah is great

Gedeon — see Gideon

Geder — wall

Gederah — sheepfold

Gederoth — sheepfolds

Gederothaim — two sheepfolds

Gedor — wall

Gehazi — valley of vision; diminisher

Gehenna — see Hell

Geliloth — circles

Gemalli — camel owner

Gemariah — Jehovah has accomplished

Gennesaret — garden of the prince-another name for the Sea of Galilee

Genubath — theft

Gera — enmity; grain

Gerah — smallest coin and weight among the Jews

Gerar — halting place

Gergesenes — people from the village of Gergesa

Gerizim — cutters; wasteland

Gershom — exile

Gershon — exile

Gershonites — inhabitants of Gershon

Geshan — firm-third son of Jahdai-also Gesham

Geshem — rain storm; corporealness-an enemy of the Jewson their return from the Exile

Geshur — bridge

Gether — a personification of an unknown people

Gethsemane — oil press

Geuel — salvation of God

Gezer — dividing

Gezerites — inhabitants of Gezer

Giah — waterfall

Gibbar — high; mighty

Gibbethon — high house

Gibea — highlander

Gibeah — hill

Gibeon — hill height

Gibeonites — inhabitants of Gibeon

Giblites — inhabitants of Gebal

Giddalti — I have magnified

Giddel — very great

Gideon — great warrior; feller of trees-see Gedeon

Gideoni — feller

Gidom — desolation

Gier-Eagel — most likely the Egyptian vulture

Gihon — gush forth

Gilalai — rolling; weighty

Gilboa — hill country

Gilead — strong; rocky; rough

Gilead, Balm of — an aromatic gum for medicinal purposes

Gilgal — rolling

Giloh — he that overturns

Gilonite — native of Giloh

Gimel — third letter in Hebrew alphabet

Gimzo — sycamore

Ginath — protection

Ginnetho — great protection

Ginnethon — great protection

Girgashites — descendants of Canaan

Girzites — inhabitants of Gezer

Gispa — listening; attentive

GittahHepher — winepress of digging

Gittaim — two winepresses

Gittites — natives of Gath

Gittith — belonging to Gath

Glede — a bird listed as unclean

Goad — a pointed rod

Goath — constancy

Gob — cistern

God — the Being perfect in power, wisdom, and goodness; the Creator and Ruler of the universe

Gog — high mountain

Golan — passage

Golgotha — skull-hill just outside Jerusalem

Goliath — an exile or soothsayer

Gomer — completion; heat

Gomorrah — submersion; ruined heap-on of the five Cities of the Plain de- stroyed along with Sodom-also Gomorrha

Goshen — drawing near

Gospel — good news

Gozan — food; quarry; place of cutting stone-Assyria deported Israel here after conquering Samaria

Greaves — amor for the leg

Gudgodah — incision

Guni — protected

Gunites — the descendants of Guni

Gur — whelp

GurBaal — dwelling place of Baal

H

Haahashtari — the courier

Habaiah — Jehovah is protection

Habakkuk — loves's embrace-a prophet in Judah during the reigns of Je- hoiakim and Josiah

Habaziniah — Jehovah's light

Habergeon — a coat of mail

Habor — fertile-a tributary of the Euphrates River

Hachaliah — Jehovah is hidden

Hachilah — gloomy

Hachmoni — the wise

Hachmonite — descendanto of Hachmoni

Hadad — the god-also Hadar

Hadadezer — (the god) Hadad is my help-also Hadarezer

HadadRimmon — Hadad and Rimmon-Aramean deities

Hadarezer — see Hadadezer

Hadashah — new

Hadassah — myrtle

Hadattah — new

Hades — see Hell

Hadid — point

Hadlai — resting

Hadoram — Hadad is high

Hadrach — dwelling

Hagab — locust

Hagabah — locust

Hagar — wandering-also Agar

Hagarites — a nation to the east of the Promised Land and which was dis- possessed by the tribe of Reuben

Hagerite — descendant of Hagar

Haggai — festive

Haggedolim — a great one

Haggeri — wanderer

Haggi — festive

Haggiah — feast of Jehovah

Haggites — see Haggi

Haggith — festal

Hai — same as Ai; near Bethel, where Abraham pitched his tent

Hakkatan — the little one

Hakkoz — the nimble

Hakupha — incitement

Halah — moist table

Halak — smooth

Halhul — tremble

Hali — sickness

Hallelujah — see Alleluia

Hallohesh — the whisperer; the slanderer-the father of one who repaired the walls of Jerusalem

Hallow — to make holy; set apart for holy use

Ham — hot

Haman — celebrated

Human (Humban)-the prime minister of Ahasuerus who plotted against the Jews

Hamath — anger; fortress

Hamathites — people of Hamath

HamathZobah — fortress of Zobah

Hammath — hot spring

Hammedatha — given by the moon

Hammelech — general title meaning "king"

Hammoleketh — the queen

Hammon — hot waters-see Hammath

HammothDor — hot spring-see Hammath

Hamonah — multitude

HamonGog — multitude of Gog

Hamor — ass-also Emmor

Hamuel — wrath of God

Hamul — pity

Hamutal — kinsman of the dew

Hanameel — gift of grace of God

Hanan — merciful

Hananeel — God is gracious

Hanani — gracious

Hananiah — Jehovah is gracious

Hanes — mercury

Hannah — grace

Hannathon — dedicated to grace

Hanniel — God is gracious-also Haniel

Hanoch — dedicated

Hanun — favored

Hapharaim — two pits

Hara — hill

Haradah — hear

Haran — mountains; strong; enlightened-also Charran

Haranite — mountaineer

Harbona — ass driver

Hareph — early born

Hareth — a forst in which David hid

Harhaiah — Jehovah is protecting

Harhas — glitter

Harhur — nobility; distinction

Harim — snub nosed

Hariph — early born

Harnepher — panting

Harod — trembling

Harodite — the home of two of David's mighty men; trembling

Haroeh — the seer

Harorite — see Harodite

Harosheth — carving

Harsha — artificer

Harum — elevated

Harumaph — slit nosed

Haruphite — a native of Hariph

Haruz — industrious

Hasadiah — Jehovah is king

Hasenuah — the violated

Hashabiah — Jehovah is associated

Hashabnah — Jehovah is a friend

Hashabniah — Jehovah is a friend

Hashbadana — judge

Hashem — shining

Hashmonah — fruitfulness

Hashub — associate

Hashubah — association

Hashum — shining

Hashupha — see Hasupha

Hasrah — glitter

Hassenaah — the thorn hedge

Hasshub — see Hashub

Hasupha — stripped

Hatach — chamberlain

Hathath — terror

Hatipha — taken; captive

Hatita — exploration

Hattil — decaying

Hattush — contender

Hauran — black land

Havilah — circle; a desert tribe

HavothJair — tent villages of Jair

Hazael — God sees

Hazaiah — Jehovah is seeing

HazarAddar — village of Addar

HazarEnan — village of fountains

HazarGaddah — town of Gadah

HazarHatticon — enclosure

HazarMaveth — court of death

HazarShual — fox village

HazarSusah — captive mares

HazarSusim — same as HazarSusah

HazazonTamar — see HazezonTamar

Hazel — almond

Hazelelponi — protection of the face of

Hazerim — villages

Hazeroth — enclosures

HazezonTamar — sandy surface of the palm tree

Haziel — God is seeing

Hazo — vision; seer

Hazor — enclosure

HazorHadattah — new Hazor

He — fifth letter of Hebrew alphabet

Heber — companion-also Eber

Hebrew — one from the other side

Hebron — friendship

Helah — tenderness

Helam — fortress

Helbah — fertile

Helbon — fat

Heldai — enduring

Heleb — fat

Heled — see Heldai

Helek — portion

Helem — strength

Heleph — passing over

Helez — vigor

Heli — climbing

Helkai — Jehovah is my portion

Helkath — part

HelkathHazzurim — field of rock

Hell — the grave; place of eternal torment

Helon — valorous

Hemam — raging

Heman — faithful

Hemath — warm

Hemdan — pleasant

Hen — favor

Hana — troubling

Henadad — Hadad is gracious

Henoch — dedicated

Hepher — pit

Hephzibah — my delight is in her

Heres — sun

Heresh — work; silence

Hermes — Mercury (the god); interpreter

Hermogenes — born of Hermes

Hermon — devoted to destruction

Hermonites — inhabitants of Hermon

Herod — heroic

Herodians — an influential Jewish party

Herodias — heroic

Herodion — heroic

Hesed — kindness

Heshbon — stronghold; reason, reckoning

Heshmon — rich soil

Heth — a personificiation of the Hittites

Hethlon — fearful dwelling

Hezeki — Jehovah is strength

Hezekiah — Jehovah is strength; strengthened of Jah-also Ezekias

Hezion — vision

Hezir — returning home

Hezrai — blooming; beautiful

Hezro — blooming

Hezron — blooming-also Esrom

Hiddai — mighty; chief

Hiddekel — sound

Hiel — God is living

Hierapolis — holy city

Higgaion — a deep sound

Hilen — grief

Hilkiah — Jehovah is protection; my portion

Hillel — praised greatly

Him — unit of measurement, equal to about one and a half gallons

Hinnom — their riches-a narrow valley southwest of Jerusalem

Hirah — distinction

Hiram — my brother is the exalted

Hizkiah — Jehovah is strength

Hizkijah — Jehovah is strength

Hobab — beloved-the father-in-law or brother-in-law of Moses

Hobah — hiding place

Hod — majesty

Hodaviah — honorer of Jehovah-also Hodaiah

Hodesh — new moon

Hodevah — honorer of Jehovah

Hobiah — splendor (or honor) of Jehovah-also Hodijah

Hoglah — partridge

Hoham — whom Jehovah

Holiness — a unique quality of divinity; consecration to God; spiritual purity

Holon — grief

Homam — see Hemam

Homer — a heap

Hophni — strong

Hor — hill

Horam — height

Horeb — desert

Horem — dedicated to God

HorHagidgad — cleft mountain

Hori — free; noble

Horim — cave dwellers-also Horites

Hormah — dedicated to God

Horonaim — double caves

Hosah — refuge

Hosanna — save, now, we beseech thee

Hosea — help; Jehovah is help-also Osee

Hosen — trousers

Hoshaiah — whom Jehovah helps

Hoshama — whom Jehovah hears

Hoshea — Jehovah is help or salvation-also Oshea, Joshua, Jehoshua

Hotham — determination-also Hothan

Hothir — abundance

Hough — to cut the tendons of a leg

Hukkok — hewn

Hukok — ditch

Hul — circle

Heldah — weasel

Humtah — place of lizards

Hupham — coast inhabitant; protected

Huppah — protection

Huppim — coast inhabitant; protection-see Hupham

Hur — free; noble

Hurai — mighty; chief-see Hiddai

Huram — same as Hiram

Huri — linen weaver

Hushah — haste

Hushai — quick

Husham — hasting; alert

Hushim — hasting; hasters

Huz — firm

Huzzab — meaning uncertain (it is decreed)

Hymenaeus — nuptial

I

I AM — a title indicating self existence; applied to God

Ibhar — chooser; Jehovah chooses-one of David's sons

Ibleam — ancient people

Ibneiah — Jehovah builds up

Ibnijah — Jehovah builds up

Ibri — one who passes over; a Hebrew

Ibsam — see Jibsam

Ibzan — famous; splendid

Ichabod — inglorious

Iconium — coming

Iconoclast — a breaker of images

Idalah — land of slander

Idbash — honey sweet

Iddo — beloved

Idumea — red; earthy-see Edom

Igal — Jehovah redeems

Igdaliah — Jehovah is great

Igeal — Jehovah redeems

Ignominy — humiliation and disgrace

Iim — heaps

IjeAbarim — ruins of Abraham

Ijon — heap; ruin

Ikkesh — subtle; crooked

Ilai — supreme

Illyricum — joy-a Roman provice of Europe

Imla — fullness

Immanuel — God (is) with us-also Emmanuel

Immer — loquacious; prominent

Imna — lugging

Imnah — lugging

Imprecation — pronouncing a curse

Imrah — height of Jehovah; stubborn

Imri — talkative; projecting

Incontinency — uncontrolled indulgence of the passions

Iphedeiah — Jehovah redeems

Ir — watcher; city

Ira — watchful

Irad — fleet

Iram — citizen

Iri — watchful

Irijah — seen of Jehovah

Irnahash — serpent city

Irpeel — God heals

IrShemesh — city of the sun

Iru — watch

Isaac — laughter-the son of Abraham and Sarah, born to them in their old age, and the father of Jacob and Esau

Isaiah — salvation of Jehovah, Jah has saved-a prophet in Israel-also Esaias

Iscah — Jehovah is looking; who looks

Ishbah — praising; appeaser

Ishbak — leaning; free

IshbiBenob — dweller at Nob

IshBosheth — man of shame

Ishhod — man of majesty

Ishi — salutary

Ishi — my husband

Ishiah — Jehovah exists

Ishijah — Jehovah exists

Ishma — high; desolate

Ishmael — God hears

Ishmaelites — descendants of Ishmael

Ishmaiah — Jehovah hears

Ishmerai — Jehovah is keeper

Ishod — man of majesty

Ishpan — he will hide

IshTob — good man

Ishuah — he will level-also Isuah

Ishuai — equal

Ismachiah — Jehovah will sustain

Ismaiah — Jehovah hears

Ispah — to lay bare

Israel — God strives

Israelites — descendants of Israel

Issachar — reward

Isshiah — Jehovah exists

Isuah — see Ishuah

Isue — see Ishuai

Ithai — being

Ithamar — land; island of palms

Ithiel — God is

Ithmah — bereavement

Ithnan — given

Ithra — abundance

Ithran — excellent

Ithream — residue of the people

Ithrite — pre-eminence

IttahKazin — gather

Ittai — timely

Iturea — mountains-a small province on the northwest boundary of Pales- tine at the base of Mount Hermon

Ivah — hamlet

Izhar — shining-also Izehar

Izharites — see Izhar - also Izeharites

Izliah — Jehovah delivers

Izrahiah — Jehovah shines

Izri — fashioner

J

Jaakan — intelligent-also Jakan

Jaakobah — to Jacob

Jaala — elevation-also Jaalah

Jaalam — hidden

Jaanai — answerer

JaareOregim — foresters

Jaasau — Jehovah makes

Jaasiel — God is maker

Jaazaniah — Jehovah is hearing

Jaaziah — Jehovah is determining

Jaaziel — God is determining

Jabal — moving

Jabbok — flowing

Jabesh — dry place

JabeshGilead — dry

Jabez — height

Jabin — intelligent; observed

Jabneel — building of God

Jachan — afflicting

Jachin — founding; he will establish

Jacinth — a sapphire stone

Jacob — supplanter; following after; heel catcher, uprooter; to take the place of by force-the son of Isaac and Rebekah and twin brother of Esau; became the father of the Jewish nation

Jada — knowing

Jadau — friend

Jaddua — very knowing; known

Jadon — judging

Jael — a wild goat

Jagur — husbandman

Jah — poetic form of Jehovah

Jahath — comfort; revival

Jahaz — a place trodden under foot; to stamp (threshing floor)

Jahaziah — Jehovah reveals

Jahaziel — God reveals

Jahdai — Jehovah leads

Jahdiel — union of God; God gives joy

Jahdo — union

Jahleel — God waits; wait for God

Jahleelites — descendants of Jahleel

Jahmai — Jehovah protects

Jahzah — see Jahaz

Jahzeel — God apportions

Jahzeelites — descendatns of Jahzeel

Jahzerah — Jehovah protects

Jahziel — God apportions

Jair — Jehovah enlightens

Jairite — descendant of Jair

Jairus — enlightened-Greek form of Jair

Jakeh — hearkening

Jakim — a setter up

Jalon — Jehovah abides

Jambres — opposer

James — Greek form of Jacob

Jamin — right hand; favor

Jaminites — descendants of Jamin

Jamlech — Jehovah rules

Janai — answer

Janna — an ancestor of Joseph, the husband of Mary

Jannai — a form of John

Jannes and Jamres — Eqyptian magicians at the time of Exodus

Janoah — resting-also Janohah

Janum — sleeping

Japheth — the extender; fair; enlarged

Japhia — enlarging

Japhlet — Jehovah causes to escape

Japhleti — to shine

Japho — beauty

Jarah — unveiler; honey

Jareb — contender; avenger

Jared — descending-also Jered

Jaresiah — Jehovah gives a couch

Jarha — the Lord nourishes

Jarib — striving

Jarmuth — height

Jaroah — new moon

Jashen — shining

Jasher — upright

Jashobeam — the people return

Jashub — turning back

JashubiLethem — turning back to Bethlehem

Jashubites — descendants of Jashub

Jasiel — God is Maker-also Jaasiel

Jason — healing

Jasper — a precious stone (quartz)

Jathniel — God is giving

Jattir — preeminence

Javan — the son of Japheth, as well as his descendants

Jazer — helpful; God helps-also Jaazer

Jaziz — shining

Jearim — woods

Jeaterai — steadfast

Jeberechiah — Jehovah is blessing; Jehovah blesses

Jebus — manager

Jebusi — trodden underfoot

Jebusites — descendants of Canaan

Jecamiah — may Jehovah

Jechoniah — see Jeconiah

Jechonias — see Jeconiah

Jecoliah — Jehovah is able

Jeconiah — Jehovah establishes

Jedaiah — Jehovah is praise

Jediael — God knows

Jedidah — beloved

Jedidiah — beloved of Jehovah

Jeduthun — a choir of praise

Jeezer — father of help-contracted form of Abiezer

Jeezerites — see Jezer

JegarSahadutha — heap of witness

Jehaleleel — God is praised

Jehdeiah — union of Jehovah

Jehezekel — God is strong

Jehiah — Jehovah is living

Jehiel — God is living

Jehizkiah — Jehovah is strong; Jeovah strengthens

Jehoadah — unveiler; honey

Jehoaddan — Jehovah gives delight

Jehoahaz — Jehovah upholds

Jehoash — see Joash

Jehohanan — Jehovah is gracious-also Johanan

Jehoiachin — Jehovah establishes

Jehoiada — Jehovah knows

Jehoiakim — Jehovah sets up; Jehovah has established

Jehoiarib — Jehovah contends

Jehonadab — Jehovah is liberal

Jehonathan — Jehovah gives

Jehoram — Jehovah is high-also Joram

Jeloshabeath — Jehovah makes oath

Jehoshaphat — Jehovah is judge-also Josaphat

Jehosheba — Jehovah makes oath

Jehoshua — see Joshua

Jehoshuah — see Joshua

Jehovah — the personal, revealed name of God translated from the He- brew consonants YHWH

JehovahJireh — the Lord will provide

JehovahNissi — the Lord is my banner

JehovahShalom — the Lord send peace

Jehozabad — Jehovah endows

Jehozadak — Jehovah is righteous

Jehu — Jehovah is he

Jehubbah — hidden

Jehucal — Jehovah is able

Jehud — praising

Jehudi — a Jew

Jehudijah — the Jewess

Jehush — see Jeush

Jeiel — God snatches away

Jekabzeel — congregation of God

Jekameam — standing of the people

Jekamiah — may Jehovah establish

Jekuthiel — God is mighty

Jemima — little dove

Jemuel — God is speaking

Jephthah — an opposer-also Jephthae

Jephunneh — appearing

Jerah — moon

Jerahmeel — God is merciful

Jerahmeelites — descendants of Jerahmeel, the great-grandson of Judah

Jered — low; flowing

Jeremai — Jehovah is high

Jeremiah — Jehovah is high-also Jeremias, Jeremy

Jeremoth — elevation

Jeriah — Jehovah is foundation-also Jerijah

Jeribai — Jehovah contends

Jericho — his sweet smell-a fortified city of Canaan conquered by the Isra- elites

Jeriel — foundation of God

Jerimoth — elevation

Jerioth — tremulousness

Jeroboam — enlarger; he pleads the people's cause

Jeroham — loved

Jerubbaal — contender with Baal

Jerubbesheth — contender with the idol

Jeruel — vision of God

Jerusalem — possession of peace; founded peaceful-the capital of Judah and city of David

Jerusha — possession

Jeshaiah — Jehovah is helper

Jeshanah — old

Jesharelah — Jehovah is joined. whom God has bound

Jeshebeab — seat of the father

Jesher — rightness

Jeshimon — solitude

Jeshishae — Jehovah is ancient; aged

Jeshohaiah — humbled by Jehovah

Jeshua — Jehovah is deliverance

Jeshuah — Jehovah is deliverance

Jeshurun — blessed

Jesimiel — God sets

Jesse — Jehovah exists; wealthy; to stand out, be conspicuous

Jesui — equal-the third son of Asher

Jesurun — blessed-a symbolic name for Israel

Jesus — Jehovah is salvation-the son of the Virgin Mary; came to earth as the Messiah and died for the salvation of His people.

Jether — preeminent

Jetheth — subjection

Jethlah — an overhanging place

Jethro — preeminence

Jetur — meaning uncertain

Jeuel — snatching away

Jeush — collector-also Jehush

Jeuz — counselor

Jezaniah — Jehovah is hearing

Jezebel — unexalted; unhusbanded

Jezer — formation

Jeziah — Jehovah unites

Jeziel — God unites

Jezliah — Jehovah delivers

Jezoar — he will shine

Jezrahiah — Jehovah is shining

Jezreel — God sows

Jezreelite — a person from Jezreel

Jibsam — lovely scent

Jidlaph — melting away

Jimna — lugging-also Jimnah

Jimnites — descendatns of Jimna

Jiphtah — breaking through

JiphthahEl — God opens

Joab — Jehovah is father

Joah — Jehovah is brother

Joahaz — Jehovah helps

Joanna — God given

Joash — Jehovah has given; Jehovah supports-also Jehoash

Joash — Jehovah has given

Joatham — Jehovah is perfect-see Jotham

Job — hated; persecuted-a pious man of Uz whose endurance in fierce trial resulted in marvelous blessing

Jobab — to call shrilly

Jochebed — Jehovah is honor or glory

Jod — tenth letter of the Hebrew alphabet

Joda — see Judah

Joed — Jehovah is witness

Joel — Jehovah is God

Joelah — God is snatching; may he avial

Joezer — Jehovah is help

Jogbehah — high

Jogli — exiled

Joha — Jehovah is living

Johanan — Jehovah is gracious

John — gift of God

Joiada — Jehovah knows

Joiakim — Jehovah sets up

Joiarib — Jehovah contends

Jokdeam — anger of the people

Jokim — Jehovah sets up

Jokmeam — revenge of the people

Jokneam — building up of the people

Jokshan — fowler

Joktan — he will be made small

Jona — a dove-also Jonas

Johadab — Jehovah is liberal

Jonah — a dove-also Jonas

Jonan — grace

Jonathan — Jehovah is given

JonathElemRechokim — the silent dove fo the far ones

Joppa — beauty-also Jopho

Jorah — early born

Jorai — rainy

Joram — Jehovah is high-also Jehoram

Jordan — the descender-a river in Palestine

Jorim — Jehovah is high

Jorkoam — spreading the people

Josabad — Jehovah endows

Josaphat — Jehovah judges

Josedech — Jehovah is righteous

Joseph — may he increase

Joses — helped-one of Jesus' brothers

Joshah — Jehovah is a gift

Joshaphat — Jehovah judges

Joshaviah — Jehovah is equality

Joshbekashah — seated in hardness

Joshua — Jehovah is salvation-also Jeshua, Jeshuah

Joshua — Jehovah saves

Josiah — Jehovah supports-also Josias

Josias — Jehovah supports-also Josiah

Josibiah — Jehovah causes to dwell

Josiphiah — Jehovah abides

Jot — Greek iota (i); Hebrew yodh (y)

Jotbah — goodness

Jotbath — goodness-also Jotbathah

Jotham — Jehovah is perfect-also Joatham

Jozabad — Jehovah endows

Jozachar — Jehovah remembers

Jozadak — Jehovah is righteous

Jubal — playing; nomad

Jubilee, Year of — the year in which slaves were set free, property was re- turned to its original owner, debts were to be forgiven, and the land was al- lowed to rest, all of which were reminders of the refreshing the Lord pro- vides His people

Jucal — Jehovah is able

Judah — praise-also Juda

Judas — praise

Judes — praise

Judea — the praise of the Lord

Judith — Jewess

Julia — soft haired

Julius — soft haired

Junia — bouncing; jolting

Juniper — a shrub of the broom family

JushabHesed — kindness is returned

Justus — just

Juttah — turning away

K

Kabzeel — the congregation of God

Kadesh — holy

KadeshBarnea — holy

Kadmiel — God the primeval; before God

Kadmonites — easterners

Kallai — Jehovah is light; swift

Kanah — of reeds

Kareah — bald head

Karka — floor; deep ground

Karkor — they rested; even or deep ground

Karnaim — horns; a city in northern Transjordan

Kartah — city

Kartan — town; city

Kattath — small

Kedar — powerful; dark

Kedemah — eastward

Kedemoth — antiquity; old age

Kedesh — holy-also (Kedesh-Naphtali)

Kehelathah — a whole; a congregation

Keilah — fortress

Kelaiah — Jehovah is light; swift for Jehovah

Kelita — littleness

Kemuel — God stands; God's mound

Kenan — acquired

Kenath — possession

Kenaz — side; hunting

Kenite — pertaining to coppersmiths

KerenHappuch — horn of antimony

Kerioth — the cities

Keros — fortress; crooked

Keturah — incense

Kezia — cassia

Keziz — the angle; border; cassia tree

KibrothHattaavah — the graves of lust

Kibzaim — double gathering

Kidron — obscure; making black or sad

Kinah — buying; dirge; lamentation

Kir — a city; wall or fortress of earthenware; meeting

KirHaraseth — city of the sun; wall of burnt brick; city of pottery (clay vessels)-a fortified city

KirHareseth — city of the sun; wall of burnt brick; city of pottery (clay vessels)-a fortified city

KirHaresh — city of the sun; wall of burnt brick; city of pottery (clay vessels)-a fortified city

KirHeres — city of the sun; wall of burnt brick; city of pottery (clay vessels)- a fortified city

Kiriathaim — double city-also Kirjathaim

Kirioth — same as Kerioth

Kirjath — city; vocation; meeting

Kirjathaim — see Kiriathaim

KirjathArba — fourth city

KirjathArim — same as Kirjath-Jearim

KiriathBaal — same as Kirjath-Jearim

KirjathJearim — city of woods-a city of the Gibeonites

KirjathSannah — city of destruction

KirjathSepher — city of books

Kish — bow; power

Kishi — snarer; fowler

Kishion — hardness

Kishon — bending; crooked-river of northern Palestine-also Kison

Kithlish — it is a wall

Kitron — making sweet

Koa — male camel

Kohath — assembly

Kohathites — descendatns of Kohath

Kolaiah — voice of Jehovah

Koph — letter of the Hebrew alphabet

Korah — baldness-also Core

Korahites — the Levites who were descendants of Korah

Kore — one who proclaims

Koz — thorn

Kushaiah — snarer; fowler

L

Laadah — order; festival

Laadan — festive born; ordered

Laban — white, glorious

Lachish — who exists of himself

Lael — belonging to God

Lahad — oppression; dark colored

LahaiRoe — of the living one who sees me

Lahmam — their bread

Lahmi — Beth-lehemite

Laish — lion

Lakum — obstruction

Lama — the Aramaic word for "Why?"

Lamech — strong youth; overthrower

Lamed — letter of the Hebrew alphabet

Laodicea — a chief city of Asia Minor

Lapidoth — flames; torches

Lasea — wise

Lasha — to anoint

Lasharon — of or to Sharon

Lazarus — God has helped-Latin form of the Hebrew name "Eleazar"

Leah — weary

Leannoth — a musical term, possibly suggesting a responsive reading or singing

Lebanah — white-also Lebana

Lebanon — white; the snow white mountain-one of two mountain ranges in northern Palestine

Lebaoth — lioness

Lebbeus — surname of Judas

Lebonah — incense

Lecah — walking; addition

Leek — an onion like plant

Lees — sediment in wine jars

Lehabim — flame; red

Lehi — jawbone

Lemuel — Godward; dedicated

Leshem — a lion-same as Laish

Letushim — sharpened

Leummim — peoples

Levi — joined

Leviathan — twisted; coiled; to writhe, weave, coil, twist, intertwine

Levites — descendants of Levi

Libertines — freedmen-Jews who had been set free from Roman slavery

Libnah — white

Libni — whiteness; distinguished

Libya — heart of the sea-the land and people west of Egypt

Likhi — learned

Linus — net

LoAmmi — not my people

Lod — nativity

Lois — pleasing; better

Lot — veiled-Abraham's nephew who excaped from wicked Sodom

Lotan — Hidden

Love — unselfish, benevolent concern for another; brotherly concern; the object of brotherly concern or affection

Low — the furthest down; deep; depressed; common; level; soft; humble

Lubim — dwellers in a thirsty land-the people who lived in the North African continent west of Egypt, now Libya

Lucas — same as Luke

Lucifer — light bearer

Lucius — morning born; of light

Lud — a personification of the Lydians-also Ludim

Luhith — made of boards

Luke — light giving-evangelist, physician, and author of the Gospel of Luke and the Book of Acts

Luz — separation

Lycaonia — she wolf-a rugged, inland district of Asia Minor

Lycia — land of Lycus

Lydia — Lydus land; native of Lydia

Lysanias — that drives away sorrow

Lysias — lame dissolution-first name "Claudius"

Lystra — that dissolves-a city of Lycaonia

M

Maacah — depression-also Maachah

Maachathites — inhabitants of Maachah

Maadai — Jehovah is ornament

Maadiah — Jehovah is ornament

Maai — Jehovah is compassionate

MaalehAcrabbim — ascent of scorpions

Maarath — den

Maaseiah — Jehovah is a refuge

Maasiai — work of Jehovah

Maath — small

Maaz — counselor

Maaziah — strength of Jehovah

Macedonia — a nation lying to the north of Greece proper

Machbanai — thick

Machbenah — knob; lump

Machi — decrease

Machir — salesman; sold

Machnadebai — liberal; gift of the noble one

Machpelah — double

Madai — a personification of the Medes

Madmannah — measure of a gift

Madmen — dunghill

Madmenah — dung heap

Madon — strife

Magbish — strong

Magdala — tower

Magdalene — of Magdala

Magdiel — God is renowned

Magi — a priestly sect in Persia

Magog — covering; roof

MagorMissabib — terror is about

Magpiash — collector of a cluster of stars; moth killer

Mahalah — tenderness

Mahalaleel — God is splendor-also Maleleel

Mahalath — mild

Mahali — see Mahlil

Mahanaim — tents

MahanehDan — tents of judgement

Maharai — hasty

Mahath — dissolution; snatching

Mahavite — probably a term used for any resident of Mahanaim

Mahazioth — visions

Maher Shalal Hash Baz — the spoil hastens, the prey speeds; hasten the booty

Mahlah — mildness; sick

Mahli — mild; sickly

Mahlon — mild; sickly

Mahol — dancer

Makaz — an end

Makheloth — congregations

Makkedah — worshiping

Maktesh — mortar

Malachi — messenger of Jehovah; my messenger

Malcham — their king

Malchiel — God is a king

Malchielites — descendants of Malchiel

Malchijah — Jehovah is king-also Malchiah, Melchiah

Malchiram — my king is exalted

MalchiShua — the king is salvation-also MelchiShua

Malchus — counselor; ruler

Maleleel — Greek form of Mahalaleel

Mallothi — Jehovah is speaking

Mallows — saltiness-perennial shrub that grows in salty marshes

Malluch — counselor; ruling

Mammon — wealth or possessions

Mamre — firmness; vigor

Manaen — comforter

Manahath — resting place

Manasseh — causing forgetfulness-also Manasses

Manasses — see Manasseh

Manassites — descendatns of manasses

Mandrake — a rhubarb like herb having narcotic qualities

Maneh — a weight; consists of 50 shekels

Manna — the name the Israelites gave to the food miraculously provided them during their wilderness wandering

Manoah — rest

Maoch — poor

Maon — place of sin

Mara — bitter

Marah — bitter

Maralah — sleep

Maranatha — our Lord, come

Marcus — see Mark

Marduk — bold

Mareshah — possession

Mark — a large hammer-a Christian convert and missionary companion of Paul, as well as the writer of the Gospel of Mark

Maroth — bitterness

Marsena — worthy

Martha — lady

Mary — strong-Greek form of Miriam

Maschil — attentive-a Hebrew term that indicates a type of psalm

Mash — one of the sons of Aram

Mashal — parable

Masrekah — whistling

Massa — burden; oracle

Massah and Meribah — temptation; quarrel

Mathusala — see Methuselah

Matred — God is pursuer; expulsion

Matri — Jehovah is watching; rainy

Mattan — gift

Mattanah — gift of Jehovah

Mattaniah — gift of Jehovah

Mattatha — gift

Mattathah — gift

Mattathias — God's gift

Mattenai — gift of Jehovah

Matthan — gift

Matthat — gift

Matthew — gift of God

Matthias — God's gift

Mattithiah — gift of Jehovah

Mattock — an agricultural instrument for digging and hoeing

Maw — the fourth stomach of rminants (divided hoof animals such as cows)

Mazzaroth — the signs of the Zodiac or a constellation

Meah — a tower

Mearah — den

Mebunnai — Jehovah is intervening

Mecherathite — a dweller in Mecharah

Medad — love

Medan — judgement

Medeba — waters of grief; water of quiet

Medes — middle land-the people and country of the Medes-also Media

Median — one from Media

Megiddo — declaring a message-also Megiddon

Mehetabel — God is doing good-also Mehetabeel

Mehida — famous

Mehis — dexterity

Meholathite — a native of Meholah

Mehujael — God is combating

Mehuman — true-also Meunim

Mehunim — one whose descendants returned

MeJarkon — the waters of Jordan

Mekonah — provision

Melatiah — Jehovah delivers

Melchi — my king

Melchiah — see Malchiah

Melchizedek — king of righteousness-also Melchisedec

Melea — full

Melech — king

Melicu — counselor; ruling

Melita — affording honey-the island of Malta, in the Mediterranean Sea

Melzar — the overseer

Mem — letter of the Hebrew alphabet

Memphis — abode of the good

Memucan — no meaning known

Menahem — conforter

Menan — meaning uncertain

Mephibosheth — idol breaker

Merab — increase

Meraiah — revelation of Jehovah

Meraioth — revelations

Merari — bitter; excited

Merarites — see Merari

Merathaim — double rebellion

Mercurius — a Roman god

Mered — rebellious

Meremoth — strong; firm

Meres — worthy

Meribah — see Massah and Meribah

MeribahKadesh — see KadeshBarnea

MeribBaal — idol breaker

Merodach — bold

MerodachBaladan — (the god) Marduk has given a son

Meron — elecations

Meronothite — citizen of Meronoth

Meroz — secret

Mesech — see Meshech

Mesha — salvation

Meshach — the shadow of the prince; who is this?

Meshech — tall-also Mesech

Meshelemiah — Jehovah repays

Meshezabeel — God delivers

Meshillemith — recompense

Meshillemoth — recompense

Meshobab — restored

Meshullam — associate; friend

Meshullemeth — friend

Mesobaite — found of Jehovah

Mesopotamia — the country between two rivers

Messiah — anointed one-the One promised by God to be the great Deliv- erer of Israel-also Messias

MethegAmmah — bridle of bondage

Methusael — man of God

Methuselah — man of a javelin-also Mathusala

Meunim — see Mehunim

Mezahab — offspring of the sining one

Miamin — see Mijamin

Mibhar — choice; youth

Mibsam — sweet odor

Mibzar — fortified

Micah — who is like Jehovah?-also Micha

Micaiah — who is like Jehovah?-also Michaiah

Michael — who is like God?

Michah — who is like Jehovah?

Michal — who is like God?

Michmash — he that strikes; hidden (from view)-also Michmas

Michmethah — the gift of a striker

Michri — Jehovah possesses

Midian — contention; brawling; contentious

Midianitess — descendants of Midian

MigdalEl — tower of God

MigdalGad — town of Judah

Migdol — tower

Migron — fear; precipice

Mijamin — fortunate-also Miamin

Mikloth — twigs; sticks

Mikneiah — Jehovah is jealous

Milalai — Jehovah is elevated

Milcah — counsel

Milcom — an Ammonite god

Miletus — scarlet-a coastal city of Asia Minor-also Miletum

Millo — fullness

Miniamin — fortunate

Minni — a people of Armenia

Minnith — prepared

Miphkad — appointed place

Mirma — height

Misgab — light

Mishael — who is what God is?

Mishal — requiring-also Misheal

Misham — impetuous; fame

Misheal — see Mishal

Mishma — fame

Mishmannah — fatness

Mispar — writing

MisrephothMaim — hot waters

Mite — the Jews' smallest coin

Mithcah — sweetness

Mithredath — given by the god Mithra

Mitylene — purity-the principal city of the island of Lesbos

Mizar — little

Mizpah — watchtower-also Mizpeh

Mizpar — see Mispar

Mizpeh — watchtower

Mizraim — the personification of Egypt

Mizzah — terror; joy

Mnason — remembering

Moab — from my father

Moabites — inhabitants of Moab

Moadiah — Jehovah is ornament-same as Maadiah

Moladah — generation

Molech — king-an Ammonite deity-also Moloch

Molid — begetter

Mollified — soothed

Moloch — see Molech

Morasthite — a native of Moresheth

Mordecai — dedicated to Mars

Moreh — stretching

Moresheth Gath — possession of Gath

Moriah — bitterness of the Lord

Moses — drawer out; one born-the great lawgiver and prophet of Israel who led his people out of bondage in Egypt

Mount Baalah — mistress-a moutain located between Exron and Jabneel

Mount BaalHermon — lord of Hermon-a mount on the eastern slope of Mount Hermon

Mount Carmel — orchard-a range of moutains about 15 miles in length in NW Palestine

Mount Ebal — stone-a mountain alongside Mount Gerizim

Mount Gaash — earthquake-a hill in the territory of Ephraim, just south of TimnathSerah

Mount Gerizim — cutters; wasteland-a high mountain in central Palestine facing Mount Ebal

Mount Gilboa — hill country-a mountain overlooking the Plain of Jezreel

Mount Hor — hill-a mountain on the boundary of Edom

Mount Horeb — desert-the range of mountains of which Mount Sinai is the chief

Mount Of Olives — a hill on the eastern border of Jerusalem opposite the Temple

Mount Seir — tempest-a mountain range through Edom from the Dead Sea south to the Elanitic Gulf

Mount Shapher — beauty-a mountain encampment during Israel's wander- ings

Mount Sinai — a bush-the mountain on which Moses received the Ten Commandments

Mount Tabor — purity-a mountian located in the northern part of the Valley of Jezreel some 5.5 miles southeast of Nazareth

Mount Zion — monument; fortress-a hill of Jerusalem

Moza — origin; offspring

Mozah — unleavened Muppims — obscurities

MuthLabben — die for the son

Myra — weep-a town of Lycia

Mysia — abominable-a province in northwestern Asia Minor

N

Naam — pleasantness

Naamah — beautiful

Naaman — pleasantness

Naamathite — an inhabitant of Naamah

Naamites — descendants of Naaman

Naarah — youthful-also Naarath

Naarai — youthful

Naashon — see Nahshon

Naasson — see Nahshon

Nabal — foolish; wicked

Naboth — a sprout

Nachon — stroke

Nachor — see Nahor

Nadab — liberal

Naggai — splendor-also Nagge

Nahalal — pasture-also Nahallal,

Nahalol Nahaliel — valley of God

Naham — comfort

Nahamani — compassionate

Naharai — snorting one-also Nahari

Nahash — oracle; serpent

Nahath — lowness

Nahbi — Jehovah is protection

Nahor — piercer-also Nachor

Nahshon — oracle-also Naashon,

Naasson Nahum — comforter-also Naum

Nain — beauty

Naioth — habitation

Naomi — pleasantness; my joy

Naphish — numerous

Naphtali — that struggles; (my) wrestling

Narcissus — meaning unknown

Nathan — gift

Nathanael — God has given

NathanMelech — king's gift

Naum — see Nahum

Nazarene — a native of Nazareth

Nazareth — sanctified

Nazarite — one especially consecrated to God

Neah — moved

Neapolis — the new city

Neariah — Jehovah drives away

Nebai — projecting

Nebaioth — husbandry

Neballat — prophecy

Nebat — cultivation

Nebo — height; high place

Nebuchadnezzar — may the god Nabu guard my boundary stones- monarch of the New Babylonian Empire

Nebushasban — Nabu delivers me

NebuzarAdan — the god Nabu has given seed

Necho — Pharaoh of Egypt who fought Josiah at Megiddo

Necromancer — one who inquires of the dead

Nedabiah — Jehovah is willing

Negev — dry; parched-denotes southern Palestine

Neginah — stringed instrument

Neginoth — same as Neginah

Nehemiah — Jehovah is consolation

Nehum — pity

Nehushta — basis; ground

Nehushtan — piece of brass

Neiel — commotion of God

Nekeb — a narrow pass

Nekoda — herdsman

Nemuel — God is speaking

Nepheg — sprout; shoot

Nephish — numerous-a tribe descended from Ishmael

Nephishesim — expansions

Nephthalim — the same as Naphtali

Nephtoah — open

Nephusim — see Nephishesim

Nepotism — putting relatives in public office

Ner — light

Nereus — lamp

Nergal — a Babylonian god of war

NergalSharezer — may the god Nergal defend the prince

Neri — whose lamp is Jehovah

Neriah — whose lamp is Jehovah

Nethaneel — God gives

Nethaniah — Jehovah gives

Nethinim — given-the name given to those who were set apart to do the menial tasks of the santuary

Netophathite — an inhabitant of Netophah

Neziah — preeminent

Nezib — standing place

Nibhaz — idol of Avites

Nibshan — prophecy

Nicanor — conqueror

Nicodemus — innocent blood

Nicolatians — an early Christian sect

Nicolas — conqueror of the people

Nicopolis — the city of victory

Nimrah — an abbreviation of BethNimrah

Nimrim — bitterness; clear water

Nimrod — valiant; strong

Nimshi — Jehovah reveals

Nineve — an early spelling of Nineveh

Nineveh — meaning unknown

Nisan — beginning

Nisroch — eagle; hawk

Nitre — carbonate of soda; lye

Noadiah — Jehovah assembles

Noah — rest

Noah — flattery; movement

Nob — prophecy; produce, fruit

Nobah — prominent

Nod — vagabond

Nodab — nobility

Noe — see Noah

Nogah — splendor

Nohah — rest

Nomad — wanderer

Noph — the Hebrew name of the Egyptian city of Memphis

Nophah — fearful

Nun — continuation; fish-also Non

Nymphas — bridegroom

O

Obadiah — servant of Jehovah

Obal — bare

Obduracy — resistance to pleadings of mercy

Obed — servant

ObedEdom — servant of (the god) Edom

Obil — camel keeper; lender

Oboth — desires

Ocran — troubler

Oded — aiding; resoter

Odious — hateful

Og — giant

Ohad — strength

Ohel — tent

Olympas — meaning uncertain

Omar — speaker; mountaineer

Omega — the last letter in the Greek alphabet

Omer — dry measure, approximately three quarts equal to one-tenth ephah

Omri — Jehovah apportions, pupil

On — sun; strength

Onam — vigorous

Onan — vigorous

Onesimus — useful

Onesiphorous — profit bringer

Ono — grief of him

Onyx — fingernail

Ophel — small white cloud

Ophir — fruitful region-son of Joktan which means "will be made litte"; a re- gion known for its gold

Ophni — wearisomeness

Ophrah — a fawn

Oracle — a revelation; a wise saying

Oreb — a raven

Oren — pine; strength

Orion — strong

Ornan — active-Jebusite from whom David bought a piece of land

Orpah — fawn; youthful freshness

Osee — Greek name for the prophet Hosea

Oshea — God saves

Ossifrage — Latin for bone breaker

Ostentatious — vain, ambitious

Ostracism — exclusion of a person from society

Ostrich — large, flightless bird; figurative of cruelty

Othni — Jehovah is power

Othniel — God is power

Ouches — woven-a filigree setting for precious stones

Ozem — strength

Ozias — Greek form of Uzziah-Jehovah is strong; my strength is Jehovah

Ozni — bright

Oznites — the descendants of Ozni

P

Paarai — revelation Jehovah

Padan — plain-an abbreviated form of PadanAram

PadanAram — plain of Aram

Padon — redemption

Pagiel — God's intervention

PahathMoab — ruler of Moab

Pai — see Pau

Palal — judge

Palestine — which is covered-region between Jordan River and Dead Sea on the east and the Mediterranean on the west-also Palestina

Pallu — distinguished-also Phallu

Palti — Jehovah delivers-also Phalti

Paltite — inhabitant of Palti; Jehovah delivers

Paltiel — God delivers-also Phaltiel

Pamphylia — a nation made up of every tribe-coastal region in South Asia Minor

Pannag — sweet

Paphos — what which boils

Papyrus — a tall marsh plant growing in the Nile River region, used for making paper

Paraclete — a helper called to one's side

Parah — increasing

Paramours — illicit lovers

Paran — beauty

Parbar — a suburb

Parmashta — stronger

Parmenas — steadfast

Parnach — gifted

Parosh — fleeing; fugitive-also Pharosh

Parshandatha — given by prayer

Parsimony — stinginess; living like a miser

Parthians — inhabitants of Parthia

Partridge — the caller-a wild bird

Paruah — blooming

Parvaim — eastern

Pasach — limping

PasDammim — boundary of blood

Paseah — limping-also Phaseah

Pashur — splitter; cleaver

Pastor — shepherd

Patara — trodden under foot

Pate — the top of the head

Pathros — persuasion of ruin

Pathrusim — the inhabitants of Pathros

Patmos — mortal

Patrobas — paternal

Pau — howling-also Pai

Paul — litte-a Pharisee who was converted and made an apostle to the Gentiles; who wrote several of the letters in the New Testament

Pauper — a person unable to support himself

Pavilion — a covered place; tent; booth

Pe — letter in the Hebrew alphabet

Pedahel — whom God redeems

Pedahzur — the rock delivers

Pedaiah — Jehovah delivers

Pekah — opening; Gos has opened the eyes

Pekahiah — Jehovah has opened (the eyes)

Pekod — visitation

Pelaiah — Jehovah is distinguished

Pelaliah — Jehovah has judged

Pelathiah — Jehovah delivers

Peleg — division-also Phalec

Pelet — deliverance

Peleth — flight; haste

Pelethites — perhas a contraction of Philistines

Pelican — the vomiter-a large, web-footed bird noted for its large pouchlike beak

Peniel — hace of God

Peninnah — coral; pearl

Pentecost — fiftieth day after Passover

Penuel — face of God

Penury — extreme poverty; destitution

Peor — opening

Perazim — lord of breaches

Peres — to split into pieces

Peresh — separate

Perez — bursting through-also Pharez

PerezUzza — a breakthrough of Uzza-also PerezUzzah

Perga — very earthy-the capital of Pamphylia

Pergamos — elevation-a leading city in Mysia in Asia Minor

Perida — separation

Perizzites — dwellers in the open country

Pernicious — destructive; wicked

Persia — cuts or divides-great empire including all of western Asia and parts of Europe and Africa

Persis — Persian

Peruda — separated

Pervert — to cause to turn away from that which is good, true, or morally right

Pestle — instrument used for pulverizing material

Peter — stone; rock-a fisherman who was called to be a disciple and apostle of Christ

Pethahiah — Jehovah opens up

Pethor — soothsayer-a town in North Mesopotamia

Pethuel — God's opening

Peulthai — Jehovah's seed

Phalec — Greek form of Peleg

Phallu — see Pallu

Phalti — see Palti

Phaltiel — God delivers

Phanuel — vision of God

Pharaoh — the great house; inhabitant of the palace-the title of the ruler of Egypt

Phares — Greek form of Perez-also Pharez

Pharezites — descendants of Perez

Pharisees — separated ones-a Jewish sect that upheld the oldest traditions of Israel at the time of Jesus

Pharosh — see Parosh

Pharpar — that produces fruit

Pharzites — descendants of Pharez

Phaseah — see Paseah

Phebe — see Phoebe

Phenic — see Phoenicia - also Phenicia

Phichol — dark water

Philadelphia brotherly love

Philemon — friendship

Philetus — amiable

Philip — lover of horses

Philippi — the same

Philistia — land of sojourners-area on southwest coast of

Palestine Philistim — plural of Philistine

Philistines — rolling; migratory-the people of Philistia

Philologus — a lover of learning

Philosopher — expounder of philosophy

Philosophy — the study of fundamental truths

Phinehas — mouth of brass

Phlegon — burning

Phoebe — shining-also Phebe

Phoenecia — purple

Phoenix — a harbor in southern Crete

Phrygia — barren-region of central Asia Minor

Phurah — beauty

Phut — bow-also Put

Phuvah — utterance-also Pua, Puah

Phygellus — fugitive

Phylactery — a charm

PiBeseth — house of Bast

PiHahiroth — the mouth

Pilate — marine dart carrier

Pildash — flame of fire

Pileha — worship

Piltai — Jehovah causes to escape

Pinon — darkness

Piram — indomitable; wild

Pirathon — princely

Pirathonite — inhabitant of Pirathon

Pisgah — a mountain peak in the Abarim range in Moab

Pisidia — pitch-a mountainous district in Asia Minor

Psion — changing

Pispah — expansion

Pithom — their mouthful

Pithon — harmless

Plat — a plot of ground

Pleiades — cluster of many stars-a constellation

Plumbline — a cord with a weight, used to determine exact uprightness

Pochereth — binding

Pontus — the sea-a coastal strip of north Asia Minor

Poratha — favored

Porcius Festus — swine like-successor to Felix

Potiphar — belonging to the sun god

PotiPherah — given of the sun god

Potsherd — a fragment of broken pottery

Praetorium — see Pretorium

Pressfat — vat into which the juice was collected when grapes were pressed

Priest — authorized minister, especially one who makes sacrificial offerings and mediates between God and man

Priscilla — ancient one-also Prisca

Prochorus — choir leader

Prophecy — inspired declaration of God's will and purpose

Prophet — inspired messenger who declares the will of God

Provender — food for animals

Prudence — wisdom applied to practical matters; caution; shrewdness

Ptolemais — hot sand-a seaport city south of Tyre

Puah — utterance-also Pua, Phuvah

Publius — common; first

Pudens — shamefaced

Puhites — family of KirjathJearim

Pul — strong

Punites — a family of the tribe of Issachar

Punon — precious stone

Pur — a lot

Purim — lots

Put — see Phut

Puteoli — sulphurous wells

Putiel — God enlightens

Pygarg — a white rumped antelope

Q

Quartus — fourth

Quaternion — a company of four soldiers

R

Raamah — trembling

Raamiah — Jehovah causes trembling

Raamses — child of the sun-also Rameses

Rabbah — great-also Rabbath

Rabbi — my master

Rabbith — great

Rabble — disorderly crowd of people

Rabboni — Aramaic form of Rabbi

RabMag — head of the Magi

RabSaris — head chamberlain

RabShakeh — head of the cupbearers

Raca — a term of insult

Rachab — see Rahab

Rachal — to whisper

Rachel — ewe-also Rahel

Raddai — Jehovah subdues; beating down

Ragau — see Reu

Raguel — another name for Jethro, the father-in-law to Moses

Rahab — violence-a woman of Jericho whose hospitality was rewarded with God's blessing-also Rachab

Rahab — the proud-a figure of speech

RahabHemShebeth — Rahab sits idle

Raham — pity; love

Rahel — see Rachel

Rakem — friendship

Rakkath — empty

Rakkon — void

Ramah — elevated; high place-also Rama

 RamathaimZophim — town where Samuel was born-see

Ramah Ramathite — an inhabitant of Ramah

RamathLehi — jawbone-location in Judah where Samson slew many Phil- istines

RamathMizpeh — place of the watchtower

Rameses — see Raamses

Ramiah — Jehovah is high-an Israelite who married a foreign wife during the Exile

Ramoth — high places; heights

RamothGilead — heights of Gilead

Rapha — fearful-also Raphah

Raphu — feared; one healed

Reaiah — Jehovah sees-also Reaia

Reba — fourth part; sprout; offspring

Rebekah — flattering-also Rebecca

Recah — uttermost part-a village inJudah

Rechab — companionship

Rechabites — descendants of Rechab

Red Sea — sea of reeds

Redeemer — one who saves others from distress; a Messianic title for Jesus

Reelaiah — returned to Palestine with Zerubbabel

Regem — friendship

RegemMelech — royal friend

Rehabiah — Jehovah is a widener

Rehob — width

Rehoboam — freer of the people-also Roboam

Rehoboth — spaces

Rehum — pity

Rei — friendly

Rekem — friendship

Remaliah — Jehovah increases; whom Jehovah has adorned

Remeth — height

Remmon — see Rimmon

RemmonMethoar — Remmon to Neah

Remphan — a name for Kiyyan, a Babylonian astral deity

Rephael — God has healed

Rephah — healing; support

Rephaiah — Jehovah is healing

Rephaim — giants; spirits of the deceased (denotes the orifinal inhabitants of a land)

Rephidim — beds

Resen — bride

Reseph — glowing stone or coal-a city near Haran

Resh — letter of the Hebrew alphabet

Resheph — the name of a Canaanite deity; meaning unknown

Reu — friendship

Reuben — behold, a son

Reubenite — descendant of Reuben

Reuel — God is his friend

Reumah — exalted

Reverence — a feeling of deep respect, love, awe, and esteem; to show feelings of respect and esteem

Rezeph — pavement

Rezia — Jehovah is pleasing

Rezin — dominion

Rezon — prince; noble

Rhegium — fracture-a town in southern Italy

Rhesa — head

Rhoda — rose

Rhodes — rose-an island off the southwest coast of Asia

Ribai — Jehovah contends

Riblah — quarrel

Rimmon — pomegranate; exalted; greatness-also Remmon

RimmonParez — pomegranates of the wrath

Rinnah — praise to God; strength

Riphath — spoken

Rissah — dew

Rithmah — noise

Rizpah — variegated; hot sone

Roboam — see Rehoboam

Rodanim — see Dodanim

Rogelim — footmen

Rohgah — outcry; alarm

RomamtiEzer — highest help

Rome — City of Romulus

Rosh — head

Rue — a pungent perennial shrub

Rufus — red

Ruhamah — pitied

Rumah — exalted

Ruth — friendship; companion

S

Sabachthani — Aramaic for "hast thou forsaken me?"

Sabaoth — Hebrew for "hosts"

Sabbath — the Jewish day of rest and worship

Sabbath Day's Journey — distance one could travel on the Sabbath (about 3,100 feet)

Sabeans — descendants of Sheba

Sabtah — striking

Sabtecha — striking

Sacar — hired

Sadducees — followers of Zadok-priestly artistocratic party; often opposed to the Pharisees

Sadoc — righteous-Greek form of Zadok

Saffron — a variety of crocus; used as a perfume or medicine

Salah — the son of Arphaxad-also Sala

Salamis — shaken-a town of Cyprus

Salathiel — Greek form of Shealtiel

Salchah — thy lifting up-also Salcah

Salem — perfect peace

Salim — path

Sallai — rejecter

Sallu — weighed; dear

Salma — strength; clothing

Salmon — strength; clothing

Salmone — peace

Salome — strength; clothing

Salu — miserable; unfortunate

Salvation — the total work of God in affecting a right relationship between manking and himself

Samaria — watch mountain; the highland(er)

Samech — letter of the Hebrew alphabet

SamgarNebo — be gracious, Nebo

Samlah — garment

Samos — full of gravel-an island off the coast of Lydia

Samothracia — of the Samians and Thracians-an island in the Aegean Sea

Samson — distinguished; strong-a judge of Israel for twenty years whose great strength made famous

Samuel — asked of God; heard of God-a prophet, and the last judge, of Is- rael

Sanballat — strong

Sansannah — branch

Saph — preserver

Saphir — delightful

Sapphira — beautiful; sapphire

Sarah — princess-also Sara and Sarai

Saraph — burning

Sardis — prince of joy-the chief city of Lydia in Asia Minor

Sardites — descendants of Sered

Sarepta — a city located midway between Tyre and Sidon

Sargon — the god Sargon has established the king(ship)

Sarid — survivor

Saron — the Greek form of Sharon

Sarsechim — chief of the eunuchs

Saruch — see Serug

Satan — adversary

Satrap — protector of the land

Satyr — he goat; hairy one

Saul — asked-the first king of Israel

Scab — blemish; natural covering of a wound; sign or plague or disease

Sceva — fitted

Schin — letter of the Hebrew alphabet

Seba — drunkard

Sebat — eleventh month of the Hebrew year

Secacah — thicket

Sechu — defense

Secundus — second

Segub — might; protection

Seir — rough; wooded; hairy

Seirath — tempest

Selah — a rock

Selah — a musical term, possibly indication an intended pause

SelaHammahLekoth — rock of divisions

Seled — exultation

Seleucia — beaten by the waves-a seaport in Syria located about 5 miles north of the mouth of the Orontes River

Sem — Greek form of Shem

Semachiah — Jehovah supports

Semei — Greek form of Shimei

Senaah — thorny

Seneh — enemy

Senir — mount of light-also Shenir

Sennacherib — (the god) Sin has substituted for my brother

Senuah — a descendant of Benjamin

Seorim — fear; distress

Sephar — scribe

Sepharad — a book descending

Sepharvaim — the two scribes-also Sepharvites

Serah — extension

Seraiah — Jehovah is prince; Jehovah has prevailed

Seraphim — burning ones; to kindle; set on fire

Sered — escape; deliverance

Serug — strength; firmness-also Saruch

Seth — compensation; sprout

Sethur — secreted; hidden

Shaalbim — place of foxes — also Shaalabbin

Shaalbonite — an inhabitant of Shaalbim

Shaaph — union; friendship

Shaaraim — gates

Shaashgaz — lover of beauty; one eager to learn

Shabbethai — sabbath born

Shachia — fame of Jehovah

Shadrach — servant of the god Sin

Shage — erring; wandering

Shaharaim — double dawn

Shahazimah — heights

Shalem — safe

Shalim — foxes

Shalisha — the third-an area near Mount Ephraim, probably northeast of Lydda

Shallecheth — a casting out

Shallum — recompenser

Shallun — recompenser-one who helped repair the wall of Jerusalem

Shalmai — Jehovah is recompenser

Shalmaneser — the god Sulman is chief

Shama — hearer

Shamariah — whom Jehovah guards

Shamed — destroyer

Shamer — preserver

Shamgar — cupbearer

Shamhuth — fame; renown

Shamir — thorn hedge

Shamma — fame; renown

Shammah — fame; renown

Shammai — celebrated

Shammoth — fame; renown

Shammua — famous-also Shammuah

Shamsherai — heroic

Shapham — youthful; vigorous

Shaphan — prudent; sly

Shaphat — judge

Shapher — bright

Sharai — Jehovah is deliverer

Shareem — see Shaaraim

Sharar — strong

Sharezer — he has protected the king-also Sherezer

Sharon — his song; a well watered garden-a plain along the coastal plain of Palestine, noted for its fertility and flowery beauty

Sharonite — an inhabitant of Sharon

Sharuhen — gracious house

Shashai — noble; free

Shashak — assaulter; runner

Shaul — variant form of Saul

Shaulites — of the tribe of Shaul

Shaveh — the plain

ShavehKiriathaim — plains Kiriathaim

Shavsha — nobility-also Shisha

Sheal — request

Shealtiel — lent by God

Sheariah — Jehovah is decider

ShearJashub — a remnant returns or shall return

Sheba — oath; covenant

Shebah — seven

Shebam — fragrance-a city east of the Jordan River

Shebaniah — Jehovah is powerful

Shebarim — hopes

Sheber — breach

Shebna — youthfulness; an overseer

Shebuel — God is renown

Shecaniah — Jehovah is a neighbor

Shechem — portion-also Sichem

Shechemites — the citizens of Shechem

Shedeur — shedder of light

Shehariah — Jehovah is the dawn

Shekinah — a word expressing the glory and presence of God

Shelah — peace

Shelanites — of the tribe of Shelah

Shelemiah — Jehovah is recompense

Sheleph — drawn out

Shelesh — might

Shelomi — Jehovah is peace

Shelomith — peacefulness-also Shelomoth

Shelumiel — God is peace

Shem — name; renown

Shema — fame; repute

Shemaah — the fame

Shemaiah — Jehovah is fame; Jehovah hears

Shemariah — whom Jehovah guards

Shemeber — splendor of heroism

Shemer — watch

Shemida — fame of knowing-also Shemidah

Sheminith — eighth

Shemiramoth — fame of the highest

Shemuel — asked of God

Shen — tooth; a pointed rock

Shenazar — ivory keeper; Sin (the god) protect

Shenir — light that sleeps-the Amorite name for Hermon

Sheol — place of the dead; pit (as a subterrainean retreat)

Shepham — wild

Shephatiah — Jehovah is judge

Shephi — unconcern-a descendant of Seir the Horite

Shepho — unconcern

Shephuphan — obscurities-a son of Benjamin

Sherah — blood relationship

Sherebiah — Jehovah is originator

Sheresh — union

Sherezer — see Sharezer

Sheshai — free; noble

Sheshan — free; noble

Sheshbazzar — O Shamash (the god) protect the father

Sheth — compensation; sprout

Shethar — star; commander

ShetharBoznai — starry splendor

Sheva — self satisfying

Shicron — drunkenness

Shiggaion — irregular

Shihon — wall of strength

Shihor — blackness; dark-the east branch of the Nile River(for the dark black mud of the Nile)

ShihorLibnath — black of whiteness

Shilhi — a warrior; one with darts

Shilhim — armed

Shillem — compensation

Shillemites — the residents of Shillem

Shiloah — sent; fountain; flowing stream

Shiloh — peace

Shiloni — weapon; armor

Shilshah — might; heroism

Shimea — fame; rumor

Shimeath — fame

Shimei — Jehovah is fame; Jehovah hear me

Shimeon — hearing

Shimhi — see Shimei

Shimi — see Shimei

Shimma — see Shammah

Shimrath — watch

Shimri — Jehovah is watching

Shimrith — watch

Shimron — watch

ShimronMeron — guard of lashing

Shimshai — Jehovah is splendor

Shinab — the king Admah

Shinar — watch of him that sleeps-the region around Babylon

Shiphi — Jehovah is fullness

Shiphmite — a native of Shiphmoth

Shiphrah — beauty

Shiphtan — judge

Shisha — distinction; nobility

Shishak — another name for Sesconchis I, king of Egypt

Shitrai — Jehovah is deciding

Shittah — the acacia tree

Shittim — thorns

Shiza — splendor

Shoa — kings

Shobab — returning

Shobach — expansion

Shobai — Jehovah is glorious

Shobal — wandering

Shobek — free

Shobi — Jehovah is glorious

Shocho — defense-also Shochoh

Shoham — leek green beryl

Shomer — keeper

Shophach — see Shoback

Shoshannim — lilies-a musical term

ShoshannimEduth — a musical term

Showbread — bread of thy face

Shubacl — God is renown-also Shebuel

Shuham — depression

Shuhamites — of the tribe of Shuham

Shuhite — a descendant of Shua

Shulamite — a native of Shulam

Shunammite — a native of Shunem

Shunem — their sleep

Shuni — fortunate

Shunites — Shuni's descendants

Shupham — obscurities-a son of Benjamin

Shuphamites — descendants of Shupham

Shuppim — serpent

Shur — wall

Shushan — a lily

ShushanEduth — lily of the testimony-a musical term

Shuthelah — setting of Telah

Sia — congregation-also Siaha

Sibbecai — Jehovah is intervening-also Sibbechai

Sibboleth — see Shebboleth

Sibmah — to be cold (cool)-known for their strong wine which would make an experienced drinker drunk very quickly

Sibraim — twofold hope

Sichem — portion

Siddim — Vale of-the tilled field

Sidon — hunting; fishery; fish market

Sidonians — of the tribe of Sidon

Signet — a seal used to give personal authority to a document

Sihon — great; bold

Sihor — blackness-also Shihor

Silas — forest; woody; third; asked-also Silvanus

Silla — exalting

Siloam — sent-also Siloah

Silvanus — see Silas

Simeon — hearing

Simeonites — descendants of Simeon

Simon — hearing

Simony — using religious offices as means of profit

Simri — Jihovah is watching-gatekeeper of the tabernacle in David's day

Sin — thoughts or behavior which are contrary to the glory or character of God; to commit an offense against God's laws

Sin — bush

Sinai — a bush-also Sina

Sinim — people from a far land, possibly from the land of Sin-also Sinites

Sion — see Zion

Siphmoth — fruitful-a place in southern Judah frequented by David

Sippai — Jehovah is preserver

Sirah — turning aside

Sirion — breastplate

Sisamai — Jehovah is distinguished

Sisera — mediation; array

Sitnah — hatred

Sivan — third month of the Jewish and Babylonian years

Sluices — aftificial passages for water, usually equipped with floodgates to measure the flow

Smyrna — myrrh

Socoh — defense

Sod — heavy with moisture; boiled; to boil; make heavy

Sodi — Jehovah determines

Sodom — their secret; to scorch; burnt-one of the five Cities of the Plain, destroyed because of its wickedness

Sodoma — see Sodom

Sodomite — a male cult prostitute; a man who practices sexual activities with other men

Solomon — peace-David's son by Bathsheba and David's successor as king of unified Israel

Sopater — one who defends the father

Sophereth — learning

Sorek — vine

Sosipater — one who defends the father

Sosthenes — strong; powerful

Sotai — Jehovah is turning aside

Sottish — thick headed

Soundness — freedom from injury or disease; firmness; stability

Stephanas — crown

Stephen — crown-a deacon who became the first Christian martyr

Suah — riches; distinction

Succoth — tents

SuccothBenoth — tabernacles of girls

Suchathites — descendants of Caleb

Sukkim — booth dwellers

Sur — rebellion

Susanchites — inhabitants of Susa of Elam

Susanna — lily

Susi — Jehovah is swift or rejoicing

Sychar — end

Sychem — shoulder, ridge

Syene — a bush

Synagogue — gathering; congregation-a house of worship for Jews follow- ing the Exile in Babylon

Syntyche — fortunate

Syracuse — that draws violently-a city on the east coast of Sicily

Syria — the highland(er)-the Aramaeans; the nation to the north and east of Israel

Syriac — language based on an Aramaic dialect

SyroPhoenician — an inhabitant of Phoenicia

T

Taanach — who humbles thee

TaanathShiloh — breaking down a fig tree

Tabbaoth — spots; rings

Tabbath — celebrated

Tabeel — God is good; pleasing to God

Taberah — burning

Tabernacle — the tent where God met with His people after the Exodus

Tabor — purity

Tabrimmon — the god Rimmon is good

Tachmonite — wise

Tadmor — bitterness

Tahan — graciousness

Tahanites — of the tribe of Tahan

Tahath — depression; humility

Tahpanhes — secret temptation-also Tehaphnehes

Tahpenes — the wife of the pharoah who received Solomon's enemy, Ha- dad

Tahrea — flight

TahtimHodshi — lowlands of Hodshi

Talebearer — one who gossips

TalithaCumi — damsel, arise

Talmai — bold; spirited

Talmon — oppressor; violent

Tamah — combat-one whose descendants returned from the Exile

Tamar — palm

Tammuz — a Babylonian god

Tanach — battlement

Tanhumeth — comfort

Taphath — ornament

Tappuah — apple; hill place

Tarah — wretch

Taralah — strength

Tarea — flight

Tarshish — hard; contemplation; smelting pot/plat; refinery-also Tharshish

Tarsus — winged-the capital of the Roman province of Cilicia

Tartak — hero of darkness

Tatnai — gift

Tau — letter in the Hebrew alphabet

Teats — breasts

Tabah — thick; strong

Tebaliah — Jehovah is protector; Jehovah has purified

Tebeth — the name of the Hebrew tenth month

Tehaphnehes — an important city in the time of Jeremiah

Tehinnah — entreaty; suppplication

Tekel — weighed

Tekoa — that is confirmed-also Tekoah

Tekoite — an inhabitant of Tekos

TelAbib — heap of new grain

Telah — vigor

Telaim — lambs-a placc in extreme southern Judah

Telassar — taking away-also Thelasar

Telem — their shadow

TelHaresha — suspension of the plow

TelHarsa — mound of workmanship

TelMelan — hill of salt

Tema — south; sunburnt

Teman — southern

Temani — tribe in northeast Edom

Temanite — an inhabitant of Teman

Temeni — fortunate

Tenons — projections in a piece of wood used to make a joint

Terah — turning; duration-also Thara

Teraphim — household idols used by neighboring tribes and by apostate Israel

Teresh — strictness; reverence

Tertius — third

Tertullus — third

Teth — letter in the Hebrew alphabet

Tetrarch — a ruler over a fourth part of a kingdom

Thaddaeus — breast

Thahash — reddish

Thamah — see Tamah

Thamar — see Tamar

Thara — see Terah

Tharshish — see Tarshish

Thebez — muddy Thelasar — see Telassar

Theophilus — loved by God

Thessalonica — victory at sea-city situated on the Macedonian coast

Theudas — the gift of God

Thimnathah — see Timnah

Thomas — twin-one of the twelve apostles of Jesus

Thummin — see Urim and Thummin

Thyatira — sacrifice of labor-an important town in the Roman provice of Asia

Tiberias — good vision-a city on the west coast of the Sea of Galilee

Tiberius — son of the river Tiber

Tibhath — extension

Tibni — intelligent

Tidal — splendor; renown

TiglathPileser — my trust is in the son of Asharra

Tikvah — hope

TilgathPilneser — see TiglathPileser

Tilon — mockery; scorn

Timaeus — honorable

Timna — alloted portion; restraining

Timnah — portion; image-also Timnath and Thimnathah

TimnathHeres — see TimnathSerah

TimnathSerah — image of the sun

Timnite — an inhabitanto of Timnah

Timon — honorable

Timotheus — see Timothy

Timothy — honored of God-a young friend and convert of Paul

Tiphsah — passage

Tiras — longing

Tirhanah — kindness

Tiria — foundation

Tirshatha — reverend-a title of the governor of Judea under Persian rule

Tirzah — delight

Tishbite — an inhabitant of Tishbeh

Titus — pleasant

Toah — depression; humility

Tob — good

Tobadonijah — the Lord Jehovah is good

Tobiah — Jehovah is good

Tochen — middle

Togarmah — all bone

Tohu — depression; humility

Toi — error; wandering-also Tou

Tola — warm; crimson

Tolad — kindred of God

Tolaites — descendants of Tola

Tophel — ruin

Tophet — a drum; smiting; contempt-a place where dead bodies are burned

Trachonitis — strong

Troas — penetrated-an important city on the coast of Mysia

Trogullium — fruit port-a rocky projection of the ridge of Mycale and a town

Trophimus — a foster child

Tryphaena — dainty

Tryphosa — delicate

Tubal — a son of Japheth and a tribe in eastern Asia Minor

TubalCain — Tubal, the smith

Tychicus — fortunate

Tyrannus — tyrant

Tyre — rock

Tzaddi — letter of the Hebrew alphabet

U

Ucal — signs of God

Uel — will of God

Ulai — pure water

Ulam — solitary; preceding

Ulla — election; burden

Ummah — darkened

Unicorn — the wild ox

Unni — answering is with Jehovah

Uphaz — pure gold

Ur — flame; light

Ur of the Chaldees — fire-city in the highlands of Mesopotamia

Urbane — pleasant, witty

Uri — enlightened; my light

Uriah — Jehovah is my light

Urias — see Uriah

Uriel — God is my light

Urijah — Jehovah is my light

Urim and Thummin — lights and perfections-priestly objects of uncertain description

Uthai — my iniquity; Jehovah is help

Uz — counsel; firmness

Uzai — hoped for

Uzal — wandering

Uzza — strength-also Uzzah

UzzenSherah — ear of the flesh

Uzzi — Jehovah is strong; my strength

Uzzia — Yahweh is strong

Uzziah — Jehovah is strong; my strength is Jehovah

Uzziel — God is my stength; God is strong

Uzzielites — members of the family of Uzziel

V

Vababond — an aimless wanderer

Vajezatha — born of Ized; given of the best one

Vaniah — praise, or nourishment, of Jehovah

Vashni — the second

Vashti — beautiful woman; best

Vau — letter in the Hebrew alphabet

Vophsi — fragrant; rich

W

Winnow — to remove chaff by a current of air; rid oneself of something un- wanted

Withes — a slender flexible branch or twig used as a band or line

Z

Zaanaim — see Zaanannim

Zaanan — pointed

Zaavan — causing fear

Zabad — endower

Zabbai — roving about; pure

Zabbud — endowed

Zabdi — Jehovah is endower

Zabdiel — my gift is God

Zabud — bestowed

Zabulon — see Zebelun

Zaccai — pure

Zaccheus — pure

Zaccur — well remembered-also Zacchur

Zachariah — memory of the Lord

Zacharias — see Zechariah

Zacher — fame

Zadok — righteous-also Sadoc

Zaham — fatness

Zain — letter of the Hebrew alphabet

Zair — small

Zalaph — purification

Zalmon — terrace; accent

Zalmonah — shade

Zalmunna — withdrawn from protection

Zamzummin — murmurers

ZaphnathPaaneah — revealer of secrets

Zaphon — north

Zara — see Zerah-also Zarah

Zareah — see Zorah

Zareathites — see Zorathite

Zared — brook

Zarephath — smelting pot

Zaretan — cooling-also Zartanah and Zarthan

ZarethSharhar — beauty of the dawn

Zarhites — descendants of the family of Zerah

Zartanah — see Zaretan-also Zarthan

Zattu — lovely; pleasant-also Zatthu

Zavan — see Zaavan

Zaza — projection

Zealot — zealous one-a party of the Jews violently opposed to the Romans-also Zealotes

Zebadiah — Jehovah is endower

Zebah — victim

Zebaim — gazelles

Zebedee — the gift of Jehovah

Zebina — bought

Zeboim — gazelles

Zebudah — endowed

Zebul — dwelling

Zebulun — dwelling; habitation

Zebulunites — natives of Zebulun

Zechariah — Jehovah is renowned; Jehovah remembers

Zedad — mountainside

Zedekiah — Jehovah is righteousness-also Zidkijah

Zeeb — wolf

Zelah — rib

Zelek — split

Zelophehad — firstborn

Zelotes — see Zealot

Zelzah — noontide

Zemaraim — wool

Zemira — song

Zenan — coldness

Zenas — living

Zephaniah — Jehovah is darkness; Jehovah has treasured

Zephath — which beholds

Zephathah — watchtower

Zepho — watch-also Zephi

Zephon — dark; wintry

Zephonites — descendants of Zepho

Zer — perplexity

Zerah — sprout-also Zara and Zarah

Zerahiah — Jehovah has come forth

Zered — see Zared

Zereda — ambush; cool-also Zeredathah

Zeresh — gold

ZerethShahar — the splendor of dawn

Zeri — balm

Zeror — bundle

Zeruah — bull breasted-mother of Jereboam I

Zerubbabel — sea of Babylon-also Zorobabel

Zeruiah — balm-mother of Joab

Zetham — shining

Zethan — olive tree

Zethar — conquerer

Zia — terrified

Ziba — plantation

Zibeon — wild robber-son of Seir

Zibia — gazelle

Zibiah — gazelle

Zichri — renowned

Ziddim — huntings

Zidkijah — see Zedekiah

Zidon — hunting-ancient city of Caanan

Zidonians — hunting-residents of Zidon

Zif — splendor; bloom

Ziha — dried

Ziklag — measure pressed down

Zilpah — myrrh dropping

Zilthai — shadow

Zimmah — counsel

Zimran — celebrated

Zimri — celebrated

Zin — swelling

Zina — fruitful

Zion — monument; fortress; set up; conspicuous; sign; pillar-one of the hills on which Jerusalem was built-also Sion

Zior — smallness

Ziph — refining place

Ziphah — lent

Ziphim — see Ziphites

Ziphion — see Zephon

Ziphites — inhabitants of Ziph

Ziphron — rejoicing

Zippor — bird

Zipporah — little bird

Zithri — Jehovah is protection

Ziz — flower

Ziza — shining; brightness

Zizah — shining; brightness

Zoan — motion; activity-main headquarters of Pharoahs; where Moses per- formed his signs

Zoar — small; to be brough low; ignoble; without honor

Zobah — station-also Zoba

Zobebah — the affable

Zohar — nobility; distinction

Zoheleth — that creeps; serpent

Zoheth — strong

Zophah — watch

Zophai — watcher-a brother of Samuel

Zophar — hairy; rough

Zophim — place for a watchman

Zorah — leprosy; wasp, hornet-also Zoreah and Zareah

Zorathite — native of Zorah and descendants of Caleb-also Zorathities

Zorobabel — see Zerubabbel

Zuar — little

Zuph — watcher

Zur — rock

Zuriel — God is my rock

Zurishaddai — the Almighty is a rock

Zuzim — prominent; giant

About the Author

Bruce D. Allen is an internationally known minister of the gospel of Jesus Christ, keynote conference speaker, and best-selling author of several highly acclaimed and anointed books, including the best-seller "Gazing into Glory". Bruce walks in and ministers from the glory realms of God with miracles and signs following. A modern-day Enoch, Bruce's mandate from the Lord Jesus is to train and equip believers to walk fully in the supernatural things of God, equipping believers to live a life of miracles, signs and wonders, moving supernaturally across the Earth for the purposes of, and the glory of the Lord. It is Bruce's passion to equip and launch believers into their full inheritance in Christ. Bruce Allen has appeared on "It's Supernatural" with Sid Roth and is also the host of the popular television program "For His Glory" on Angel TV.

OTHER BOOKS BY BRUCE D. ALLEN

Gazing into Glory

Prophetic Promise of the Seventh Day

Promise of the Third Day

Biblical Secrets of a Supernatural Life

Foundations of Glory

Translation by Faith

Gazing into Glory Workbook

What's in a Name

Available at Still Waters International Missions,
Amazon.com and Bookstores worldwide.

Made in the USA
Columbia, SC
02 November 2025